PRESSING ON
Through
It All

PRESSING ON
Through It All

Scriptural Encouragement
For These Last Days

WARREN B. SMITH

Mountain Stream Press
Magalia, California

Mountain Stream Press
P.O. Box 1794
Magalia, CA 95954

Publisher's Cataloging-in-Publication Data
Smith, Warren B.
  PRESSING ON THROUGH IT ALL: Scriptural encouragement for these last days
/ Warren B. Smith.
    pages cm

  ISBN 978-0-9978982-8-6 (softbound : alk. paper) 1. Christianity and encouragement--scripture verses 2. King James Version

Printed in the United States of America

For all those who love God's Word
And look to it for comfort and hope
in these challenging times.

Contents

NOTE TO THE READER

As former members of the New Age movement, my wife Joy and I have spent the last thirty-three years actively warning about the deceptive teachings of the New Age/New Spirituality that have progressively crept into the church. For the last ten years, to offset the spiritual heaviness that often accompanies this kind of ministry, I would study, compile, and then arrange certain Scriptures around specific themes that would provide my wife and I with encouragement and spiritual uplift. Almost as an afterthought, these personal studies became small booklets that were made available to share with others. I used the theme "through it all" for each of the booklets, hoping people reading them would find the same scriptural encouragement we had received from them.

In writing these "through it all" booklets, Joy and I knew we had to be prepared to face the testing that would likely come with such a project. But little did we know that the testing would unfold as it did. Yet, we have marveled at how the Lord has sustained us and carried us through this difficult period.

Over the last year and a half, we had to cut down and remove well over a hundred dead trees on our property that had become casualties of a recent four-year drought. Then one year ago today, we were suddenly displaced from our home——and remain displaced as of this writing—by a destructive house fire that also resulted in the deaths of four of our beloved cats. Living in a number of different locations since the fire—many of them motels—we still await the restoration of our home. Adding to this and a number of other challenging events, I underwent three unexpected emergency surgeries after a life that had been virtually free of any medical concerns whatsoever.

As a result of all of these trying circumstances, we soon found ourselves reading our own "through it all" booklets for encouragement and support—*Trusting God Through It All, Standing Fast Through It All, Praising God Through It All,* along with all the other booklets. And they have given us immeasurable comfort and strength during this demanding time. Now combined in one book, I pray these carefully selected scriptural compilations will provide you with the same degree of comfort and strength they have given us.

God's Word is truly awesome and encouraging, and oh so necessary, as we all endeavor to keep pressing on—through it all.

—Warren B. Smith
July 3, 2017

PRESSING ON THROUGH IT ALL

Through temptations great and small,
Remaining faithful through it all.
Tho' heresies into the church may crawl,
We keep God's Word through it all.

Through it all, through it all,
Pressing on, to God's higher call.

Betrayed by friends, we still stand tall,
Trusting God, through it all.
Through persecutions, what'ere befall,
Standing fast, through it all.

Through it all, through it all
Pressing on, to God's higher call.

Tho' the enemy surrounds us with darkened pall,
We rejoice in the Lord, through it all.
Even when our backs are up against the wall,
We praise God, through it all.

Through it all, through it all
Pressing on, to God's higher call.

While the world parties and has a ball,
We watch and pray, through it all.
And our Saviour's words we do recall,
"Look up, and lift up your heads," through it all.

Through it all, through it all
Pressing on, to God's higher call.

—WBS

CHAPTER ONE

Praying Through It All

PRAYER

Prayer was appointed to convey
The blessings God designs to give;
Long as they live should Christians pray;
For only when they pray they live.

And shall we in dead silence lie,
When Christ stands waiting for our prayer?
My soul, thou hast a Friend on high;
Arise and try thy interest there.
If pain afflict, or wrongs oppress;
If cares distract, or fears dismay;
If guilt deject, if sin distress;
The remedy's before thee—Pray!

Depend on Christ, thou canst not fail;
Make all thy wants and wishes known.
Fear not; His merits must prevail;
Ask what thou wilt; it shall be done!

—Joseph Hart[1]

E. M. Bounds (1835-1913) authored a number of classic books on prayer. A former attorney who became a preacher, editor, author, and intercessory prayer warrior, Bounds reputedly arose at four each morning and prayed for three hours. In his book *The Necessity of Prayer*, Bounds wrote:

> God's Word is a record of prayer—of praying men and their achievements, of the Divine warrant of prayer and of the encouragement given to those who pray.[2]

He described the urgency of prayer as:

> . . . a mighty movement of the soul toward God. It is a stirring of the deepest forces of the soul, toward the throne of heavenly grace. It is the ability to hold on, press on, and wait. Restless desire, restful patience, and strength of grasp are all embraced in it. It is not an incident, or a performance, but a passion of soul. It is not a want, half-needed, but a sheer necessity.[3]

He further wrote:

> Nothing distinguishes the children of God so clearly and strongly as prayer. It is the one infallible mark and test of being a Christian. Christian people are prayerful, the worldly-minded, prayerless. Christians call on God; worldlings ignore God, and call not on His Name. But even the Christian had need to cultivate continual prayer. Prayer must be habitual, but much more than a habit. It is duty, yet one which rises far above, and goes beyond the ordinary implications of the term. It is the expression of a relation to God, a yearning for Divine communion.[4]

JESUS OUR MEDIATOR

Scripture tells us Jesus Christ is the one mediator between God and man (1 Timothy 2:5) and that we are to take everything to God through Him in prayer. He is our Lord, our Savior, and our Friend.

WHAT A FRIEND WE HAVE IN JESUS

What a Friend we have in Jesus,
All our sins and griefs to bear!
What a privilege to carry,
Everything to God in prayer!
O what peace we often forfeit,
O what needless pain we bear,
All because we do not carry
Everything to God in prayer!

Have we trials and temptations?
Is there trouble anywhere?
We should never be discouraged—
Take it to the Lord in prayer.
Can we find a friend so faithful,
Who will all our sorrows share?
Jesus knows our every weakness;
Take it to the Lord in prayer.

Are we weak and heavy laden,
Cumbered with a load of care?
Precious Saviour, still our refuge—
Take it to the Lord in prayer.
Do thy friends despise, forsake thee?
Take it to the Lord in prayer!
In His arms He'll take and shield thee,
Thou wilt find a solace there.

Blessed Saviour, Thou hast promised—
Thou wilt all our burdens bear;
May we ever, Lord, be bringing,
All to Thee in earnest prayer.
Soon in glory bright, unclouded,
There will be no need for prayer—
Rapture, praise, and endless worship
Will be our sweet portion there.

—Joseph M. Scriven (1855)

BIBLICAL PRAYER

PRAY TO GOD

Seek ye the LORD while he may be found, call ye upon him while he is near. (Isaiah 55:6)

Thus saith the LORD the maker thereof, the LORD that formed it, to establish it; the LORD is his name; Call unto me, and I will answer thee, and show thee great and mighty things, which thou knowest not. (Jeremiah 33:2-3)

PRAY GOD'S WILL BE DONE

And this is the confidence that we have in him, that, if we ask any thing according to his will, he heareth us: And if we know that he hear us, whatsoever we ask, we know that we have the petitions that we desired of him. (1 John 5:14-15)

Teach me to do thy will; for thou art my God: thy spirit is good; lead me into the land of uprightness. (Psalm 143:10)

PRAY IN JESUS NAME

For there is one God, and one mediator between God and men, the man Christ Jesus; Who gave himself a ransom for all, to be testified in due time. (1 Timothy 2:5-6)

And whatsoever ye shall ask in my name, that will I do, that the Father may be glorified in the Son. If ye shall ask any thing in my name, I will do it. (John 14:13-14)

Verily, verily, I say unto you, Whatsoever ye shall ask the Father in my name, he will give it you. Hitherto have ye asked nothing in my name: ask, and ye shall receive, that your joy may be full. (John 16:23-24)

PRAY AND ABIDE IN JESUS

If ye abide in me, and my words abide in you, ye shall ask what ye will, and it shall be done unto you. (John 15:7)

WATCH AND PRAY

Watch and pray, that ye enter not into temptation: the spirit indeed is willing, but the flesh is weak. (Matthew 26:41)

But the end of all things is at hand: be ye therefore sober, and watch unto prayer. (1 Peter 4:7)

And take heed to yourselves, lest at any time your hearts be overcharged with surfeiting, and drunkenness, and cares of this life, and so that day come upon you unawares. For as a snare shall it come on all them that dwell on the face of the whole earth. Watch ye therefore, and pray always, that ye may be accounted worthy to escape all these things that shall come to pass, and to stand before the Son of man. (Luke 21:34-36)

PRAY IN THE MORNING

Give ear to my words, O LORD, consider my meditation. Hearken unto the voice of my cry, my King, and my God: for unto thee will I pray. My voice shalt thou hear in the morning, O LORD; in the morning will I direct my prayer unto thee, and will look up. (Psalm 5:1-3)

PRAY MORNING, NOON, AND EVENING

As for me, I will call upon God; and the LORD shall save me. Evening, and morning, and at noon, will I pray, and cry a loud: and he shall hear my voice. (Psalm 55:16-17)

PRAY EVERYWHERE

I will therefore that men pray every where, lifting up holy hands, without wrath and doubting. (1 Timothy 2:8)

PRAY CONTINUALLY

Let love be without dissimulation. Abhor that which is evil; cleave to that which is good. Be kindly affectioned one to another with brotherly love; in honour preferring one another; Not slothful in business; fervent in spirit; serving the Lord; Rejoicing in hope; patient in tribulation; continuing instant in prayer. (Romans 12:9-12)

PRAY UNCEASINGLY

Rejoice evermore. Pray without ceasing. (1 Thessalonians 5:16-17)

PRAY ALWAYS

And he spake a parable unto them to this end, that men ought always to pray, and not to faint. (Luke 18:1)

PRAY WITH STRIVING

Now I beseech you, brethren, for the Lord Jesus Christ's sake, and for the love of the Spirit, that ye strive together with me in your prayers to God for me. (Romans 15:30)

PRAY WITH FAITH

Jesus answered and said unto them, Verily I say unto you, If ye have faith, and doubt not, ye shall not only do this which is done to the fig tree, but also if ye shall say unto this mountain, Be thou removed, and be thou cast into the sea; it shall be done.

And all things, whatsoever ye shall ask in prayer, believing, ye shall receive. (Matthew 21:21-22)

But without faith it is impossible to please him: for he that cometh to God must believe that he is, and that he is a rewarder of them that diligently seek him. (Hebrews 11:6)

PRAY HUMBLY

If my people, which are called by my name, shall humble themselves, and pray, and seek my face, and turn from their wicked ways; then will I hear from heaven, and will forgive their sin, and will heal their land. (2 Chronicles 7:14)

PRAY BOLDLY

Seeing then that we have a great high priest, that is passed into the heavens, Jesus the Son of God, let us hold fast our profession. For we have not an high priest which cannot be touched with the feeling of our infirmities; but was in all points tempted like as we are, yet without sin. Let us therefore come boldly unto the throne of grace, that we may obtain mercy, and find grace to help in time of need. (Hebrews 4:14-16)

According to the eternal purpose which he purposed in Christ Jesus our Lord: In whom we have boldness and access with confidence by the faith of him. (Ephesians 3:11-12)

PRAY FERVENTLY

The effectual fervent prayer of a righteous man availeth much. (James 5:16)

PRAY AND SING PRAISES

And at midnight Paul and Silas prayed, and sang praises unto God: and the prisoners heard them. And suddenly there was a great earthquake, so that the foundations of the prison were shaken: and immediately all the doors were opened, and every one's bands were loosed. (Acts 16:25-26)

PRAY WITH THANKSGIVING

Be careful for nothing; but in every thing by prayer and supplication with thanksgiving let your requests be made known unto God. And the peace of God, which passeth all understanding, shall keep your hearts and minds through Christ Jesus. (Philippians 4:6-7)

Continue in prayer, and watch in the same with thanksgiving. (Colossians 4:2)

PRAY FOR ONE ANOTHER

Confess your faults one to another, and pray one for another, that ye may be healed. (James 5:16)

PRAY FOR YOUR ENEMIES

But I say unto you, Love your enemies, bless them that curse you, do good to them that hate you, and pray for them which despitefully use you, and persecute you; That ye may be the children of your Father which is in heaven: for he maketh his sun to rise on the evil and on the good, and sendeth rain on the just and on the unjust. For if ye love them which love you, what reward have ye? do not even the publicans the same? (Matthew 5:44-46)

PRAY FOR ALL MEN

I exhort therefore, that, first of all, supplications, prayers, intercessions, and giving of thanks, be made for all men; For kings, and for all that are in authority; that we may lead a quiet and peaceable life in all godliness and honesty. For this is good and acceptable in the sight of God our Saviour; Who will have all men to be saved, and to come unto the knowledge of the truth. (1 Timothy 2:1-4)

PRAY IN PRIVATE

And when thou prayest, thou shalt not be as the hypocrites are: for they love to pray standing in the synagogues and in the corners of the streets, that they may be seen of men. Verily I say unto you, They have their reward. But thou, when thou prayest, enter into thy closet, and when thou hast shut thy door, pray to thy Father which is in secret; and thy Father which seeth in secret shall reward thee openly. (Matthew 6:5-6)

PRAY WITHOUT REPETITION

But when ye pray, use not vain repetitions, as the heathen do: for they think that they shall be heard for their much speaking. Be not ye therefore like unto them: for your Father knoweth what things ye have need of, before ye ask him. (Matthew 6:7-8)

PRAY WITH FORGIVENESS

Therefore I say unto you, What things soever ye desire, when ye pray, believe that ye receive them, and ye shall have them. And when ye stand praying, forgive, if ye have ought against any: that your Father also which is in heaven may forgive you your trespasses. But if ye do not forgive, neither will your Father which is in heaven forgive your trespasses. (Mark 11:24-26)

PRAY FOR FORGIVENESS

If we say that we have no sin, we deceive ourselves, and the truth is not in us. If we confess our sins, he is faithful and just to forgive us our sins, and to cleanse us from all unrighteousness. (1 John 1:8-9)

PRAY WITH CRYING AND STRONG TEARS

So also Christ glorified not himself to be made an high priest; but he that said unto him, Thou art my Son, to day have I begotten thee. As he saith also in another place, Thou art a priest for ever after the order of Melchisedec. Who in the days of his flesh, when he had offered up prayers and supplications with strong crying and tears unto him that was able to save him from death, and was heard in that he feared; Though he were a Son, yet learned he obedience by the things which he suffered; And being made perfect, he became the author of eternal salvation unto all them that obey him. (Hebrews 5:5-9)

PRAY BEING RIGHTEOUS

The LORD is far from the wicked: but he heareth the prayer of the righteous. (Proverbs 15:29)

For the eyes of the Lord are over the righteous, and his ears are open unto their prayers: but the face of the Lord is against them that do evil. (1 Peter 3:12)

PRAY BEING UPRIGHT

The sacrifice of the wicked is an abomination to the LORD: but the prayer of the upright is his delight. (Proverbs 15:8)

PRAY FOR WISDOM

If any of you lack wisdom, let him ask of God, that giveth to all men liberally, and upbraideth not; and it shall be given him. But let him ask in faith, nothing wavering. For he that wavereth is like a wave of the sea driven with the wind and tossed. For let not that man think that he shall receive any thing of the Lord. (James 1:5-7)

PRAY THE LORD'S PRAYER

After this manner therefore pray ye: Our Father which art in heaven, Hallowed be thy name. Thy kingdom come. Thy will be done in earth, as it is in heaven. Give us this day our daily bread. And forgive us our debts, as we forgive our debtors. And lead us not into temptation, but deliver us from evil: For thine is the kingdom, and the power, and the glory, for ever. Amen. (Matthew 6:9-13)

PRAY AND FAST

And they said unto him, Why do the disciples of John fast often, and make prayers, and likewise the disciples of the Pharisees; but thine eat and drink? And he said unto them, Can ye make the children of the bridechamber fast, while the bridegroom is with them? But the days will come, when the bridegroom shall be taken away from them, and then shall they fast in those days. (Luke 5:33-35)

Then came the disciples to Jesus apart, and said, Why could not we cast him out? And Jesus said unto them, Because of your unbelief: for verily I say unto you, If ye have faith as a grain of mustard seed, ye shall say unto this mountain, Remove hence to yonder place; and it shall remove; and nothing shall be impossible unto you. Howbeit this kind goeth not out but by prayer and fasting. (Matthew 17:19-21)

PRAY TO BE KEPT FROM ENEMY DEVICES

Keep me from the snares which they have laid for me, and the gins of the workers of iniquity. (Psalm 141:9)

PRAY FOR DELIVERANCE FROM PERSECUTION

My times are in thy hand: deliver me from the hand of mine enemies, and from them that persecute me. Make thy face to shine upon thy servant: save me for thy mercies' sake. (Psalm 31:15-16)

O LORD my God, in thee do I put my trust: save me from all them that persecute me, and deliver me. (Psalm 7:1)

Attend unto my cry; for I am brought very low: deliver me from my persecutors; for they are stronger than I. (Psalm 142:6)

PRAY WITH THE HOLY SPIRIT INTERCEDING

Likewise the Spirit also helpeth our infirmities: for we know not what we should pray for as we ought: but the Spirit itself maketh intercession for us with groanings which cannot be uttered. And he that searcheth the hearts knoweth what is the mind of the Spirit, because he maketh intercession for the saints according to the will of God. (Romans 8:26-27)

But ye, beloved, building up yourselves on your most holy faith, praying in the Holy Ghost, Keep yourselves in the love of God, looking for the mercy of our Lord Jesus Christ unto eternal life. (Jude 1:20-21)

PRAY WITH ALL PERSEVERANCE AND SUPPLICATION IN THE SPIRIT

Praying always with all prayer and supplication in the Spirit, and watching there unto with all perseverance and supplication for all saints. (Ephesians 6:18)

PRAY FOR LABORERS

But when he saw the multitudes, he was moved with compassion on them, because they fainted, and were scattered abroad, as sheep having no shepherd. Then saith he unto his disciples, The harvest truly is plenteous, but the labourers are few; Pray ye therefore the Lord of the harvest, that he will send forth labourers into his harvest. (Matthew 9:36-38)

And judgment is turned away backward, and justice standeth afar off: for truth is fallen in the street, and equity cannot enter. Yea, truth faileth; and he that departeth from evil maketh himself a prey: and the LORD saw it, and it displeased him that there was no judgment. And he saw that there was no man, and wondered that there was no intercessor, therefore his arm brought salvation unto him; and his righteousness, it sustained him. (Isaiah 59:14-16)

PRAY FOR DOORS OF OPPORTUNITY

Withal praying also for us, that God would open unto us a door of utterance, to speak the mystery of Christ, for which I am also in bonds. That I may make it manifest, as I ought to speak. (Colossians 4:3-4)

PRAY THAT GOD'S WORD HAS FREE COURSE

Finally, brethren, pray for us, that the word of the Lord may have free course, and be glorified, even as it is with you. (2 Thessalonians 3:1)

PRAY NOT TO BE PRIDEFUL

Let not the foot of pride come against me, and let not the hand of the wicked remove me. (Psalm 36:11)

PRAY TO BE PROVEN

Examine me, O LORD, and prove me; try my reins and my heart. (Psalm 26:2)

Search me, O God, and know my heart: try me, and know my thoughts: And see if there be any wicked way in me, and lead me in the way everlasting. (Psalm 139:23-24)

PRAY FOR HELP

Help me, O LORD my God: O save me according to thy mercy. (Psalm 109:26)

O LORD, I am oppressed; undertake for me. (Isaiah 38:14)

Give us help from trouble: for vain is the help of man. (Psalm 60:11)

PRAY FOR MERCY

Have mercy upon me, O LORD, for I am in trouble, (Psalm 31:9)

Turn thee unto me, and have mercy upon me; for I am desolate and afflicted. The troubles of my heart are enlarged: O bring thou me out of my distresses. (Psalm 25:16-17)

Hear, O LORD, and have mercy upon me: LORD, be thou my helper. (Psalm 30:10)

PRAY THAT WE RECOGNIZE OUR FRAILTY AND VANITY

LORD, make me to know mine end, and the measure of my days, what it is; that I may know how frail I am. Behold, thou hast made my days as an handbreadth; and mine age is as nothing before thee: verily every man at his best state is altogether vanity. (Psalm 39:4-5)

PRAY CONCERNING UNBELIEF

Jesus said unto him, If thou canst believe, all things are possible to him that believeth. And straightway the father of the child cried out, and said with tears, Lord, I believe; help thou mine unbelief. (Mark 9:23-24)

PRAY TO BE SAVED

For whosoever shall call upon the name of the Lord shall be saved. (Romans 10:13)

PRAY TO BE LED BY THE LORD

For thou art my rock and my fortress; therefore for thy name's sake lead me, and guide me. (Psalm 31:3)

Teach me thy way, O LORD, and lead me in a plain path, because of mine enemies. (Psalm 27:11)

O send out thy light and thy truth: let them lead me; let them bring me unto thy holy hill, and to thy tabernacles. (Psalm 43:3)

PRAY GOD WOULD ORDER YOUR STEPS

Order my steps in thy word: and let not any iniquity have dominion over me. (Psalm 119:133)

PRAY FOR STRENGTH THROUGH GOD'S WORD

My soul melteth for heaviness: strengthen thou me according unto thy word. (Psalm 119:28)

PRAY TO BE QUICKENED THROUGH GOD'S WORD

Quicken me, O LORD, for thy name's sake: for thy righteousness' sake bring my soul out of trouble. (Psalm 143:11)

I am afflicted very much: quicken me, O LORD, according unto thy word. (Psalm 119:107)

PRAY FOR CLEANSING

Have mercy upon me, O God, according to thy lovingkindness: according unto the multitude of thy tender mercies blot out my transgressions. Wash me thoroughly from mine iniquity, and cleanse me from my sin. For I acknowledge my transgressions: and my sin is ever before me. (Psalm 51:1-3)

PRAY FOR A RIGHT SPIRIT

Create in me a clean heart, O God; and renew a right spirit within me. Cast me not away from thy presence; and take not thy holy spirit from me. Restore unto me the joy of thy salvation; and uphold me with thy free spirit. Then will I teach transgressors thy ways; and sinners shall be converted unto thee. (Psalm 51:10-13)

PRAY FOR ACCEPTABILITY

Let the words of my mouth, and the meditation of my heart, be acceptable in thy sight, O LORD, my strength, and my redeemer. (Psalm 19:14)

PRAY FOR JERUSALEM

Pray for the peace of Jerusalem: they shall prosper that love thee. (Psalm 122:6)

PRAY FOR GOD'S PEACE

The LORD bless thee, and keep thee: The LORD make his face shine upon thee, and be gracious unto thee: The LORD lift up his countenance upon thee, and give thee peace. (Numbers 6:24-26)

PRAYER FOR THE CHURCH

For this cause I bow my knees unto the Father of our Lord Jesus Christ, Of whom the whole family in heaven and earth is named, That he would grant you, according to the riches of his glory, to be strengthened with might by his Spirit in the inner man; That Christ may dwell in your hearts by faith; that ye, being rooted and grounded in love, May be able to comprehend with all saints what is the breadth, and length, and depth, and height; And to know the love of Christ, which passeth knowledge, that ye might be filled with all the fulness of God. Now unto him that is able to do exceeding abundantly above all that we ask or think, according to the power that worketh in us, Unto him be glory in the church by Christ Jesus throughout all ages, world without end. Amen. (Ephesians 3:14-21)

CHAPTER TWO

TRUSTING GOD
THROUGH IT ALL

Trusting God, for a serious Christian, means trusting the God of the Holy Bible. And the Bible is very explicit about who God is and how and why He is worthy of our complete and total trust. He is the God of Abraham, Isaac, and Jacob (Matthew 22:32). He is the One who created the world and all living things (Genesis 1:1). He loved the world so much that He sent His Son Jesus Christ into the world that whosoever believes in Him can have everlasting life (John 3:16). His attributes, works, commandments, and teachings are clearly put forth in Scripture. However, our Spiritual Adversary is continually challenging and attempting to change God's teachings and our understanding of who God is. In so doing, this deceiver's ultimate purpose is to undermine our trust in the God of the Bible.

Scripture records that when Jesus was tempted in the wilderness, He resisted the Devil's temptations by standing on God's Word. "It is written" was Jesus' straightforward rebuttal to Satan's twisted proposals. And when questioned or reproached by others, our response as believers should always be the same (Psalm 119:42). Whatever the cost and without any compromise, we are to trust God in all that we do and say. John H. Sammis' 1887 hymn *Trust and Obey* reminds us that the only way to be happy in Jesus is to trust and obey.

When we walk with the Lord
In the light of His Word,
What a glory He sheds on our way!
While we do His good will,
He abides with us still,
And with all who will trust and obey.
Trust and obey,
For there's no other way
To be happy in Jesus,
But to trust and obey.

Louisa Stead's hymn—*Tis So Sweet to Trust in Jesus* (1882)—helps us remember that we trust in Jesus by just taking Him at His Word:

Tis so sweet to trust in Jesus,
Just to take Him at His Word;
Just to rest upon His promise;
Just to know, Thus saith the Lord.
Jesus, Jesus, how I trust Him!
How I've proved Him o'er and o'er!
Jesus, Jesus, precious Jesus!
O for grace to trust Him more!

Surely, it is easy to trust in God when things are going well, but we must continue that trust when things are not going so well. The following selected Bible verses affirm why we need to maintain our trust in God—both in season and out of season.

TRUST GOD

TRUST GOD

They that trust in the LORD shall be as mount Zion, which cannot be removed, but abideth for ever. As the mountains are round about Jerusalem, so the LORD is round about his people from henceforth even for ever. (Psalm 125:1-2)

For thou art my hope, O Lord GOD: thou art my trust from my youth. By thee have I been holden up from the womb: thou art he that took me out of my mother's bowels: my praise shall be continually of thee. (Psalm 71:5-6)

Into thine hand I commit my spirit: thou hast redeemed me, O LORD God of truth. I have hated them that regard lying vanities: but I trust in the LORD. (Psalm 31:5)

Stand in awe, and sin not: commune with your own heart upon your bed, and be still. Selah. Offer the sacrifices of righteousness, and put your trust in the LORD. (Psalm 4:4-5)

TRUST GOD AND BE KNOWN BY GOD

The LORD is good, a strong hold in the day of trouble; and he knoweth them that trust in him. (Nahum 1:7)

TRUST GOD'S WORD

So shall I have wherewith to answer him that reproacheth me: for I trust in thy word. (Psalm 119:42)

TRUST GOD'S SON

That we should be to the praise of his glory, who first trusted in Christ. In whom ye also trusted, after that ye heard the word of truth, the gospel of your salvation: in whom also after that ye believed, ye were sealed with that holy Spirit of promise, Which is the earnest of our inheritance until the redemption of the purchased possession, unto the praise of his glory. (Ephesians 1:12-14)

TRUST GOD'S NAME

For our heart shall rejoice in him, because we have trusted in his holy name. (Psalm 33:21)

And they that know thy name will put their trust in thee: for thou, LORD, hast not forsaken them that seek thee. (Psalm 9:10)

I will also leave in the midst of thee an afflicted and poor people, and they shall trust in the name of the LORD. (Zephaniah 3:12)

He shall not strive, nor cry; neither shall any man hear his voice in the streets. A bruised reed shall he not break, and smoking flax shall he not quench, till he send forth judgment unto victory. And in his name shall the Gentiles trust. (Matthew 12:19-21)

TRUST GOD'S HOLINESS

But thou art holy, O thou that inhabitest the praises of Israel. Our fathers trusted in thee: they trusted, and thou didst deliver them. They cried unto thee, and were delivered: they trusted in thee, and were not confounded. (Psalm 22:3-5)

TRUST GOD WITH ALL YOUR HEART

Trust in the LORD with all thine heart; and lean not unto thine own understanding. In all thy ways acknowledge him, and he shall direct thy paths. (Proverbs 3:5-6)

TRUST GOD AND COMMIT THY WAY UNTO HIM

Delight thyself also in the LORD; and he shall give thee the desires of thine heart. Commit thy way unto the LORD; trust also in him; and he shall bring it to pass. (Psalm 37:4-5)

TRUST GOD AND HIS GOODNESS

Oh how great is thy goodness, which thou hast laid up for them that fear thee; which thou hast wrought for them that trust in thee before the sons of men! (Psalm 31:19)

TRUST GOD'S MERCY

But I am like a green olive tree in the house of God: I trust in the mercy of God for ever and ever. (Psalm 52:8)

Many sorrows shall be to the wicked: but he that trusteth in the LORD, mercy shall compass him about. (Psalm 32:10)

But I have trusted in thy mercy; my heart shall rejoice in thy salvation. I will sing unto the LORD, because he hath dealt bountifully with me. (Psalm 13:5-6)

TRUST GOD'S STRENGTH

Trust ye in the LORD for ever: for in the LORD JEHOVAH is everlasting strength. (Isaiah 26:4)

TRUST GOD OUR ROCK

The LORD is my rock, and my fortress, and my deliverer; my God, my strength, in whom I will trust; my buckler, and the horn of my salvation, and my high tower. (Psalm 18:2)

The God of my rock; in him will I trust: he is my shield, and the horn of my salvation, my high tower, and my refuge, my saviour; thou savest me from violence. (2 Samuel 22:3)

TRUST GOD AS OUR REFUGE AND FORTRESS

I will say of the LORD, He is my refuge and my fortress: my God; in him will I trust. (Psalm 91:2)

My goodness, and my fortress; my high tower, and my deliverer; my shield, and he in whom I trust; who subdueth my people under me. (Psalm 144:2)

TRUST GOD OUR SHIELD

Every word of God is pure: he is a shield unto them that put their trust in him. (Proverbs 30:5)

TRUST GOD OUR BUCKLER

As for God, his way is perfect; the word of the LORD is tried: he is a buckler to all them that trust in him. (2 Samuel 22:31)

TRUST GOD AND THE SHELTER OF HIS WINGS

I will abide in thy tabernacle for ever: I will trust in the covert of thy wings. Selah. (Psalm 61:4)

How excellent is thy lovingkindness, O God! therefore the children of men put their trust under the shadow of thy wings. (Psalm 36:7)

He shall cover thee with his feathers, and under his wings shalt thou trust: his truth shall be thy shield and buckler. (Psalm 91:4)

TRUST GOD AND NOT BE AFRAID

In God have I put my trust: I will not be afraid what man can do unto me. (Psalm 56:11)

Behold, God is my salvation; I will trust, and not be afraid: for the LORD JEHOVAH is my strength and my song; he also is become my salvation. (Isaiah 12:2)

Be merciful unto me, O God: for man would swallow me up; he fighting daily oppresseth me. Mine enemies would daily swallow me up: for they be many that fight against me, O thou most High. What time I am afraid, I will trust in thee. (Psalm 56:1-3)

He shall not be afraid of evil tidings: his heart is fixed, trusting in the LORD. (Psalm 112:7)

TRUST GOD IN PRAYER

Cause me to hear thy lovingkindness in the morning; for in thee do I trust: cause me to know the way wherein I should walk; for I lift up my soul unto thee. (Psalm 143:8)

Preserve me, O God: for in thee do I put my trust. (Psalm 16:1)

O my God, I trust in thee: let me not be ashamed, let not mine enemies triumph over me. (Psalm 25:2)

In thee, O LORD, do I put my trust: let me never be put to confusion. (Psalm 71:1)

But mine eyes are unto thee, O GOD the Lord: in thee is my trust; leave not my soul destitute. (Psalm 141:8)

TRUST GOD AND BE HELPED

The LORD is my strength and my shield; my heart trusted in him, and I am helped: therefore my heart greatly rejoiceth; and with my song will I praise him. (Psalm 28:7)

Ye that fear the LORD, trust in the LORD: he is their help and their shield. (Psalm 115:11)

TRUST GOD AND BE DELIVERED FROM THE WICKED

And the LORD shall help them, and deliver them: he shall deliver them from the wicked, and save them, because they trust in him. (Psalm 37:40)

Evil shall slay the wicked: and they that hate the righteous shall be desolate. The LORD redeemeth the soul of his servants: and none of them that trust in him shall be desolate. (Psalm 34:21-22)

TRUST GOD AND BE SAVED

Show thy marvellous lovingkindness, O thou that savest by thy right hand them which put their trust in thee from those that rise up against them. (Psalm 17:7)

And the LORD shall help them, and deliver them: he shall deliver them from the wicked, and save them, because they trust in him. (Psalm 37:40)

TRUST GOD–NOT MAN

It is better to trust in the LORD than to put confidence in man. (Psalm 118:8)

Thus saith the LORD; Cursed be the man that trusteth in man, and maketh flesh his arm, and whose heart departeth from the LORD. (Jeremiah 17:5)

TRUST GOD–NOT FRIENDS OR GUIDES

Trust ye not in a friend, put ye not confidence in a guide: keep the doors of thy mouth from her that lieth in thy bosom. For the son dishonoureth the father, the daughter riseth up against her mother, the daughter in law against her mother in law; a man's enemies are the men of his own house. Therefore I will look unto the LORD; I will wait for the God of my salvation: my God will hear me. (Micah 7:5-7)

Take ye heed every one of his neighbour, and trust ye not in any brother: for every brother will utterly supplant, and every neighbour will walk with slanders. And they will deceive every one his neighbour, and will not speak the truth: they have taught their tongue to speak lies, and weary themselves to commit iniquity. Thine habitation is in the midst of deceit; through deceit they refuse to know me, saith the LORD. (Jeremiah 9:4-6)

TRUST GOD AND NOT OURSELVES

But we had the sentence of death in ourselves, that we should not trust in ourselves, but in God which raiseth the dead: Who delivered us from so great a death, and doth deliver: in whom we trust that he will yet deliver us. (2 Corinthians 1:9-10)

He that is of a proud heart stirreth up strife: but he that putteth his trust in the LORD shall be made fat. He that trusteth in his own heart is a fool: but whoso walketh wisely, he shall be delivered. (Proverbs 28:25-26)

And such trust have we through Christ to God-ward: Not that we are sufficient of ourselves to think any thing as of ourselves; but our sufficiency is of God. (2 Corinthians 3:4-5)

TRUST GOD AND NOT WEALTH

Charge them that are rich in this world, that they be not highminded, nor trust in uncertain riches, but in the living God, who giveth us richly all things to enjoy. (1 Timothy 6:17)

TRUST GOD AND BE SAFE

The fear of man bringeth a snare: but whoso putteth his trust in the LORD shall be safe. (Proverbs 29:25)

TRUST GOD AND DO GOOD

Trust in the LORD, and do good; so shalt thou dwell in the land, and verily thou shalt be fed. (Psalm 37:3)

TRUST GOD AND DECLARE HIS WORKS

But it is good for me to draw near to God: I have put my trust in the Lord GOD, that I may declare all thy works. (Psalm 73:28)

TRUST GOD AND REJOICE

But let all those that put their trust in thee rejoice: let them ever shout for joy, because thou defendest them: let them also that love thy name be joyful in thee. (Psalm 5:11)

TRUST GOD AND BE GLAD

The righteous shall be glad in the LORD, and shall trust in him; and all the upright in heart shall glory. (Psalm 64:10)

TRUST GOD AND BE HAPPY

He that handleth a matter wisely shall find good: and whoso trusteth in the LORD, happy is he. (Proverbs 16:20)

TRUST GOD IN ALL CIRCUMSTANCES

O LORD my God, in thee do I put my trust: save me from all them that persecute me, and deliver me. (Psalm 7:1)

Though he slay me, yet will I trust in him. (Job 13:15)

For therefore we both labour and suffer reproach, because we trust in the living God, who is the Saviour of all men, specially of those that believe. (1 Timothy 4:10)

TRUST GOD AT ALL TIMES

Trust in him at all times; ye people, pour out your heart before him: God is a refuge for us. (Psalm 62:8)

TRUST GOD AND BE BLESSED

O taste and see that the LORD is good: blessed is the man that trusteth in him. (Psalm 34:8)

Blessed is that man that maketh the LORD his trust, and respecteth not the proud, nor such as turn aside to lies. (Psalm 40:4)

Blessed is the man that trusteth in the LORD, and whose hope the LORD is. For he shall be as a tree planted by the waters, and that spreadeth out her roots by the river, and shall not see when heat cometh, but her leaf shall be green; and shall not be careful in the year of drought, neither shall cease from yielding fruit. (Jeremiah 17:7-8)

TRUST GOD AND BE KEPT IN PEACE

Thou wilt keep him in perfect peace, whose mind is stayed on thee: because he trusteth in thee. (Isaiah 26:3)

TRUST GOD FOREVER

Trust ye in the LORD for ever: for in the LORD JEHOVAH
is everlasting strength. (Isaiah 26:4)

TRUSTING JESUS

The 1876 hymn, *Trusting Jesus*, written by Edgar P. Stites and put to music by pastor Dwight Moody's music minister, Ira D. Sankey, says it all. Trusting Jesus through it all. Trusting Jesus that is all.

TRUSTING JESUS

Simply trusting every day,
Trusting through a stormy way;
Even when my faith is small,
Trusting Jesus, that is all.
Brightly doth His Spirit shine,
Into this poor heart of mine.
While He leads I cannot fall,
Trusting Jesus, that is all.
Singing if my way is clear,
Praying if the path be drear.
If in danger, for Him call,
Trusting Jesus, that is all.
Trusting Him while life shall last,
Trusting Him till earth be past;
'Til I hear His final call,
Trusting Jesus, that is all.
Trusting as the moments fly,
Trusting as the days go by;
Trusting Him what - e'er befall,
Trusting Jesus, that is all.

CHAPTER THREE

WATCHFUL AND DISCERNING THROUGH IT ALL

CHRISTIAN, SEEK NOT YET REPOSE (1836)

Christian seek not yet repose,
Cast thy dreams of ease away;
Thou art in the midst of foes: Watch and pray.

Watch as if that alone were the issue of the day;
Pray that help may be sent down: Watch and pray.

—Charlotte Elliot & William H. Monk

LEARN TO DISCERN

Learn to discern, Watch and pray;
Night's almost here, Far spent is the day.

Learn to discern, Watch and pray;
Armor on tight, Keeping the enemy at bay.

Learn to discern, Watch and pray;
Don't be deceived, Narrow is the way.
If you learn to discern, To watch and pray;
Then close to Jesus You will always stay.

—WBS

The following selected verses emphasize the importance of being watchful and discerning.

WATCHFUL

BE WATCHFUL

Be watchful, and strengthen the things that remain, that are ready to die: for I have not found thy works perfect before God. Remember therefore how thou hast received and heard, and hold fast, and repent. If therefore thou shalt not watch, I will come on thee as a thief, and thou shalt not know what hour I will come upon thee. (Revelation 3:2-3)

But in all things approving ourselves as the ministers of God, in much patience, in afflictions, in necessities, in distresses, In stripes, in imprisonments, in tumults, in labours, in watchings, in fastings. (2 Corinthians 6:4-5)

Prepare the table, watch in the watchtower, eat, drink: arise, ye princes, and anoint the shield. For thus hath the Lord said unto me, Go, set a watchman, let him declare what he seeth. (Isaiah 21:5-6)

WATCH AND PRAY WITH SUPPLICATION AND PERSEVERANCE

Praying always with all prayer and supplication in the Spirit, and watching thereunto with all perseverance and supplication for all saints. (Ephesians 6:18)

WATCH AND PRAY WITH THANKSGIVING

Continue in prayer, and watch in the same with thanksgiving. (Colossians 4:2)

WATCH AND BE SOBER

For when they shall say, Peace and safety; then sudden destruction cometh upon them, as travail upon a woman with child; and they shall not escape. But ye, brethren, are not in darkness, that that day should overtake you as a thief. Ye are all the children of light, and the children of the day: we are not of the night, nor of darkness. Therefore let us not sleep, as do others; but let us watch and be sober. (1 Thessalonians 5:3-6)

But the end of all things is at hand: be ye therefore sober, and watch unto prayer. (1 Peter 4:7)

Be sober, be vigilant; because your adversary the devil, as a roaring lion, walketh about, seeking whom he may devour: Whom resist stedfast in the faith, knowing that the same afflictions are accomplished in your brethren that are in the world. (1 Peter 5:8-9)

WATCH AND PRAY REGARDING TEMPTATION

Watch and pray, that ye enter not into temptation: the spirit indeed is willing, but the flesh is weak. (Matthew 26:41)

WATCH AND STAND FAST

Watch ye, stand fast in the faith, quit you like men, be strong. (1 Corinthians 16:13)

WATCH FOR GRIEVOUS WOLVES

For I know this, that after my departing shall grievous wolves enter in among you, not sparing the flock. Also of your own selves shall men arise, speaking perverse things, to draw away disciples after them. Therefore watch, and remember, that by the space of three years I ceased not to warn every one night and day with tears. (Acts 20:29-31)

WATCH IN ALL THINGS

Preach the word; be instant in season, out of season; reprove, rebuke, exhort with all longsuffering and doctrine. For the time will come when they will not endure sound doctrine; but after their own lusts shall they heap to themselves teachers, having itching ears; And they shall turn away their ears from the truth, and shall be turned unto fables. But watch thou in all things, endure afflictions, do the work of an evangelist, make full proof of thy ministry. (2 Timothy 4:2-5)

WATCH AND PRAY ALWAYS

For as a snare shall it come on all them that dwell on the face of the whole earth. Watch ye therefore, and pray always, that ye may be accounted worthy to escape all these things that shall come to pass, and to stand before the Son of man. (Luke 21:35-36)

WATCH FOR THE LORD

Watch ye therefore: for ye know not when the master of the house cometh, at even, or at midnight, or at the cockcrowing, or in the morning: Lest coming suddenly he find you sleeping. And what I say unto you I say unto all, Watch. (Mark 13:35-37)

Blessed are those servants, whom the lord when he cometh shall find watching: verily I say unto you, that he shall gird himself, and make them to sit down to meat, and will come forth and serve them. (Luke 12:37)

Watch therefore: for ye know not what hour your Lord doth come. But know this, that if the goodman of the house had known in what watch the thief would come, he would have watched, and would not have suffered his house to be broken up. Therefore be ye also ready: for in such an hour as ye think not the Son of man cometh. (Matthew 24:42-44)

Behold, I come as a thief. Blessed is he that watcheth, and keepeth his garments, lest he walk naked, and they see his shame. (Revelation 16:15)

DISCERNING

NINEVITES COULDN'T DISCERN BETWEEN THEIR RIGHT AND LEFT HANDS

And should not I spare Nineveh, that great city, wherein are more than sixscore thousand persons that cannot discern between their right hand and their left hand. (Jonah 4:11)

DISCERNMENT IS A SIGN OF MATURITY

But strong meat belongeth to them that are of full age, even those who by reason of use have their senses exercised to discern both good and evil. (Hebrews 5:14)

DISCERNMENT IS PLEASING TO GOD

In Gibeon the LORD appeared to Solomon in a dream by night: and God said, Ask what I shall give thee. And Solomon said . . . Give therefore thy servant an understanding heart to judge thy people, that I may discern between good and bad: for who is able to judge this thy so great a people? And the speech pleased the Lord, that Solomon had asked this thing. And God said unto him, Because thou hast asked this thing, and hast not asked for thyself long life; neither hast asked riches for thyself, nor hast asked the life of thine enemies; but hast asked for thyself understanding to discern judgment. Behold, I have done according to thy words: lo, I have given thee a wise and an understanding heart; so that there was none like thee before thee, neither after thee shall any arise like unto thee. (1 Kings 3:5-6, 9-12)

THE WORD OF GOD DISCERNS THOUGHTS AND HEARTS

For the word of God is quick, and powerful, and sharper than any twoedged sword, piercing even to the dividing asunder of soul and spirit, and of the joints and marrow, and is a discerner of the thoughts and intents of the heart. (Hebrews 4:12)

SEARCH THE SCRIPTURES DAILY

These were more noble than those in Thessalonica, in that they received the word with all readiness of mind, and searched the scriptures daily, whether those things were so. (Acts 17:11)

STUDY TO SHOW YOURSELF APPROVED

Study to show thyself approved unto God, a workman that needeth not to be ashamed, rightly dividing the word of truth. (2 Timothy 2:15)

APPROVE THINGS THAT ARE EXCELLENT

And this I pray, that your love may abound yet more and more in knowledge and in all judgment; That ye may approve things that are excellent; that ye may be sincere and without offence till the day of Christ. (Philippians 1:9-10)

FEAR OF THE LORD IS THE BEGINNING OF KNOWLEDGE, WISDOM, UNDERSTANDING

My son, if thou wilt receive my words, and hide my commandments with thee; So that thou incline thine ear unto wisdom, and apply thine heart to understanding; Yea, if thou criest after knowledge, and liftest up thy voice for understanding; If thou seekest her as silver, and searchest for her as for hid treasures; Then shalt thou understand the fear of the LORD, and find the knowledge of God. (Proverbs 2:1-5)

LOVE INSTRUCTION, WISDOM, AND KNOWLEDGE

Whoso loveth instruction loveth knowledge: but he that hateth reproof is brutish. (Proverbs 12:1)

HOLY SPIRIT WILL TEACH YOU ALL THINGS

But the anointing which ye have received of him abideth in you, and ye need not that any man teach you: but as the same anointing teacheth you of all things, and is truth, and is no lie, and even as it hath taught you, ye shall abide in him. (1 John 2:27)

DRAW NIGH TO GOD

Draw nigh to God, and he will draw nigh to you. (James 4:8)

TRUST IN THE LORD AND ACKNOWLEDGE HIM

Trust in the LORD with all thine heart; and lean not unto thine own understanding. In all thy ways acknowledge him, and he shall direct thy paths. (Proverbs 3:5-6)

CALL UNTO GOD

Call unto me, and I will answer thee, and show thee great and mighty things, which thou knowest not. (Jeremiah 33:3)

PRAY FOR UNDERSTANDING

I am thy servant; give me understanding, that I may know thy testimonies. (Psalm 119:125)

ASK FOR WISDOM

If any of you lack wisdom, let him ask of God, that giveth to all men liberally, and upbraideth not; and it shall be given him. (James 1:5)

SEEK GOD'S WILL

I can of mine own self do nothing: as I hear, I judge: and my judgment is just; because I seek not mine own will, but the will of the Father which hath sent me. (John 5:30)

PROVE GOD'S WILL

And be not conformed to this world: but be ye transformed by the renewing of your mind, that ye may prove what is that good, and acceptable, and perfect, will of God. (Roman 12:2)

PROVE ALL THINGS

Prove all things; hold fast that which is good. (1 Thessalonians 5:21)

BEWARE OF FALLING FROM YOUR OWN STEADFASTNESS

Ye therefore, beloved, seeing ye know these things before, beware lest ye also, being led away with the error of the wicked, fall from your own stedfastness. (2 Peter 3:17)

EXAMINE YOURSELVES

Examine yourselves, whether ye be in the faith; prove your own selves. (2 Corinthians 13:5)

BRING ALL THOUGHTS INTO CAPTIVITY

For though we walk in the flesh, we do not war after the flesh: (For the weapons of our warfare are not carnal, but mighty through God to the pulling down of strong holds;) Casting down imaginations, and every high thing that exalteth itself against the knowledge of God, and bringing into captivity every thought to the obedience of Christ. (2 Corinthians 10:3-5)

LOVE NOT THE WORLD

Love not the world, neither the things that are in the world. If any man love the world, the love of the Father is not in him. For all that is in the world, the lust of the flesh, and the lust of the eyes, and the pride of life, is not of the Father, but is of the world. And the world passeth away, and the lust thereof: but he that doeth the will of God abideth for ever. (1 John 2:15-17)

ABHOR THAT WHICH IS EVIL

Let love be without dissimulation. Abhor that which is evil; cleave to that which is good. (Romans 12:9)

WALK NOT IN THE COUNSEL OF THE UNGODLY

Blessed is the man that walketh not in the counsel of the ungodly, nor standeth in the way of sinners, nor sitteth in the seat of the scornful. But his delight is in the law of the LORD; and in his law doth he meditate day and night. (Psalm 1:1-2)

UNDERSTAND THE TIMES

And of the children of Issachar, which were men that had understanding of the times, to know what Israel ought to do. (1 Chronicles 12:32)

DISCERN THE EVIL OF TODAY

Take therefore no thought for the morrow: for the morrow shall take thought for the things of itself. Sufficient unto the day is the evil thereof. (Matthew 6:34)

DISCERN BETWEEN THE RIGHTEOUS AND THE WICKED

Then they that feared the LORD spake often one to another: and the LORD hearkened, and heard it, and a book of remembrance was written before him for them that feared the LORD, and that thought upon his name. And they shall be mine, saith the LORD of hosts, in that day when I make up my jewels; and I will spare them, as a man spareth his own son that serveth him. Then shall ye return, and discern between the righteous and the wicked, between him that serveth God and him that serveth him not. (Malachi 3:16-18)

DISCERN BETWEEN THE SACRED AND THE PROFANE

And they shall teach my people the difference between the holy and profane, and cause them to discern between the unclean and the clean. (Ezekiel 44:23)

OVERCOME EVIL WITH GOOD

Be not overcome of evil, but overcome evil with good. (Romans 12:21)

BE AWARE OF SATAN'S DEVICES

Lest Satan should get an advantage of us: for we are not ignorant of his devices. (2 Corinthians 2:11)

KNOW THE WHOLE WORLD WILL BE DECEIVED

And the great dragon was cast out, that old serpent, called the Devil, and Satan, which deceiveth the whole world: he was cast out into the earth, and his angels were cast out with him. (Revelation 12:9)

And the light of a candle shall shine no more at all in thee; and the voice of the bridegroom and of the bride shall be heard no more at all in thee: for thy merchants were the great men of the earth; for by thy sorceries were all nations deceived. (Revelation 18:23)

TAKE HEED THAT NO MAN DECEIVE YOU

And Jesus answered and said unto them, Take heed that no man deceive you. (Matthew 24:4)

BEWARE OF MEN

But beware of men: for they will deliver you up to the councils, and they will scourge you in their synagogues. (Matthew 10:17)

BEWARE OF MEN'S TRADITIONS

Beware lest any man spoil you through philosophy and vain deceit, after the tradition of men, after the rudiments of the world, and not after Christ. (Colossians 2:8)

BEWARE OF CUNNINGLY DEVISED FABLES

For we have not followed cunningly devised fables, when we made known unto you the power and coming of our Lord Jesus Christ, but were eyewitnesses of his majesty. (2 Peter 1:16)

BEWARE OF SCIENCE FALSELY SO-CALLED

Laying up in store for themselves a good foundation against the time to come, that they may lay hold on eternal life. O Timothy, keep that which is committed to thy trust, avoiding profane and vain babblings, and oppositions of science falsely so called: Which some professing have erred concerning the faith. (1 Timothy 6:19-21)

BEWARE OF THOSE WHO PERVERT THE GOSPEL

I marvel that ye are so soon removed from him that called you into the grace of Christ unto another gospel: Which is not another; but there be some that trouble you, and would pervert the gospel of Christ. But though we, or an angel from heaven, preach any other gospel unto you than that which we have preached unto you, let him be accursed. As we said before, so say I now again, If any man preach any other gospel unto you than that ye have received, let him be accursed. (Galatians 1:6-9)

BEWARE OF EVIL MEN AND SEDUCERS

But evil men and seducers shall wax worse and worse, deceiving, and being deceived. But continue thou in the things which thou hast learned and hast been assured of, knowing of whom thou hast learned them. (2 Timothy 3:13-14)

BEWARE OF UNGODLY MEN WHO CREEP INTO THE CHURCH UNAWARES

For there are certain men crept in unawares, who were before of old ordained to this condemnation, ungodly men, turning the grace of our God into lasciviousness, and denying the only Lord God, and our Lord Jesus Christ. (Jude 1:4)

BEWARE OF FALSE PROPHETS AND FALSE TEACHERS

Beware of false prophets, which come to you in sheep's clothing, but inwardly they are ravening wolves. (Matthew 7:15)

But there were false prophets also among the people, even as there shall be false teachers among you, who privily shall bring in damnable heresies, even denying the Lord that bought them, and bring upon themselves swift destruction. And many shall follow their pernicious ways; by reason of whom the way of truth shall be evil spoken of. (2 Peter 2:1-2)

BEWARE OF FALSE APOSTLES

For such are false apostles, deceitful workers, transforming themselves into the apostles of Christ. And no marvel; for Satan himself is transformed into an angel of light. (2 Corinthians 11:13-14)

BEWARE OF FALSE CHRISTS

And Jesus answered and said unto them, Take heed that no man deceive you. For many shall come in my name, saying, I am Christ; and shall deceive many. (Matthew 24:4-5)

And many false prophets shall rise, and shall deceive many. (Matthew 24:11)

BEWARE OF HERE IS CHRIST, OR THERE; BELIEVE IT NOT

Then if any man shall say unto you, Lo, here is Christ, or there; believe it not. For there shall arise false Christs, and false prophets, and shall show great signs and wonders; insomuch that, if it were possible, they shall deceive the very elect. Behold, I have told you before. (Matthew 24:23-25)

BEWARE OF EVERY WINDBLOWN DOCTRINE

That we henceforth be no more children, tossed to and fro, and carried about with every wind of doctrine, by the sleight of men, and cunning craftiness, whereby they lie in wait to deceive; But speaking the truth in love, may grow up into him in all things, which is the head, even Christ. (Ephesians 4:14-15)

NOT CARRIED ABOUT BY STRANGE DOCTRINES

Be not carried about with divers and strange doctrines. (Hebrews 13:9)

BEWARE OF THOSE WHO DO NOT ENDURE SOUND DOCTRINE

For the time will come when they will not endure sound doctrine; but after their own lusts shall they heap to themselves teachers, having itching ears; And they shall turn away their ears from the truth, and shall be turned unto fables. (2 Timothy 4:3-4)

BEWARE OF FALSE DOCTRINE

How is it that ye do not understand that I spake it not to you concerning bread, that ye should beware of the leaven of the Pharisees and of the Sadducees? Then understood they how that he bade them not beware of the leaven of bread, but of the doctrine of the Pharisees and of the Sadducees. (Matthew 16:11-12)

BEWARE OF SEDUCING SPIRITS AND DOCTRINES OF DEVILS

Now the Spirit speaketh expressly, that in the latter times some shall depart from the faith, giving heed to seducing spirits, and doctrines of devils. (1 Timothy 4:1)

BEWARE OF ANOTHER JESUS, SPIRIT, GOSPEL

For if he that cometh preacheth another Jesus, whom we have not preached, or if ye receive another spirit, which ye have not received, or another gospel, which ye have not accepted, ye might well bear with him. (2 Corinthians 11:4)

TEST THE SPIRITS

Beloved, believe not every spirit, but try the spirits whether they are of God: because many false prophets are gone out into the world. Hereby know ye the Spirit of God: Every spirit that confesseth that Jesus Christ is come in the flesh is of God: And every spirit that confesseth not that Jesus Christ is come in the flesh is not of God: and this is that spirit of antichrist, whereof ye have heard that it should come; and even now already is it in the world. (1 John 4:1-3)

DON'T MEDDLE WITH THOSE WHO ARE INTO CHANGE

My son, fear thou the LORD and the king: and meddle not with them that are given to change: For their calamity shall rise suddenly; and who knoweth the ruin of them both? (Proverbs 24:21-22)

MARK THOSE WHO CAUSE DIVISIONS

Now I beseech you, brethren, mark them which cause divisions and offences contrary to the doctrine which ye have learned; and avoid them. For they that are such serve not our Lord Jesus Christ, but their own belly; and by good words and fair speeches deceive the hearts of the simple. (Romans 16:17-18)

REMEMBER THE SIMPLICITY OF CHRIST

But I fear, lest by any means, as the serpent beguiled Eve through his subtlety, so your minds should be corrupted from the simplicity that is in Christ. (2 Corinthians 11:3)

ABIDE IN THE DOCTRINE OF CHRIST

Whosoever transgresseth, and abideth not in the doctrine of Christ, hath not God. He that abideth in the doctrine of Christ, he hath both the Father and the Son. If there come any unto you, and bring not this doctrine, receive him not into your house, neither bid him God speed: For he that biddeth him God speed is partaker of his evil deeds. (2 John 1:9-11)

WALK IN TRUTH

I have no greater joy than to hear that my children walk in truth. (3 John 1:4)

KEEP THE WORD

But he said, Yea rather, blessed are they that hear the word of God and keep it. (Luke 11:28)

COUNT THE COST

For which of you, intending to build a tower, sitteth not down first, and counteth the cost, whether he have sufficient to finish it? (Luke 14:28)

BE WILLING TO SUFFER

For unto you it is given in the behalf of Christ, not only to believe on him, but also to suffer for his sake. (Philippians 1:29)

KNOW YOU WILL BE PERSECUTED

Yea, and all that will live godly in Christ Jesus shall suffer persecution. (2 Timothy 3:12)

KNOW YOU WILL BE HATED

And ye shall be hated of all men for my name's sake: but he that endureth to the end shall be saved. (Matthew 10:22)

KNOW YOU WILL BE CALLED BEELZEBUB/SATAN

The disciple is not above his master, nor the servant above his lord. It is enough for the disciple that he be as his master, and the servant as his lord. If they have called the master of the house Beelzebub, how much more shall they call them of his household? (Matthew 10:24-25)

BE NOT FEARFUL

For God hath not given us the spirit of fear; but of power, and of love, and of a sound mind. (2 Timothy 1:7)

BE NOT TERRIFIED

And in nothing terrified by your adversaries: which is to them an evident token of perdition, but to you of salvation, and that of God. (Philippians 1:28)

DO NOT GIVE PLACE TO THE DEVIL

Neither give place to the devil. (Ephesians 4:27)

SHAKE THE DUST OFF YOUR FEET

And whosoever shall not receive you, nor hear your words, when ye depart out of that house or city, shake off the dust of your feet. (Matthew 10:14)

GIRD UP YOUR MIND

Wherefore gird up the loins of your mind, be sober, and hope to the end for the grace that is to be brought unto you at the revelation of Jesus Christ. (1 Peter 1:13)

RESIST THE DEVIL

Be sober, be vigilant; because your adversary the devil, as a roaring lion, walketh about, seeking whom he may devour: Whom resist stedfast in the faith, knowing that the same afflictions are accomplished in your brethren that are in the world. (1 Peter 5:8-9)

PUT ON THE WHOLE ARMOUR OF GOD

Finally, my brethren, be strong in the Lord, and in the power of his might. Put on the whole armour of God, that ye may be able to stand against the wiles of the devil. For we wrestle not against flesh and blood, but against principalities, against powers, against the rulers of the darkness of this world, against spiritual wickedness in high places. Wherefore take unto you the whole armour of God, that ye may be able to withstand in the evil day, and having done all, to stand. (Ephesians 6:10-13)

HOLD FAST

Hold fast the form of sound words, which thou hast heard of me, in faith and love which is in Christ Jesus. (2 Timothy 1:13)

But that which ye have already hold fast till I come. (Revelation 2:25)

STAND FAST

If thou faint in the day of adversity, thy strength is small. (Proverbs 24:10)

ENTER THE STRAIT GATE

Enter ye in at the strait gate: for wide is the gate, and broad is the way, that leadeth to destruction, and many there be which go in thereat: Because strait is the gate, and narrow is the way, which leadeth unto life, and few there be that find it. (Matthew 7:13-14)

KEEP PRESSING ON

Brethren, I count not myself to have apprehended: but this one thing I do, forgetting those things which are behind, and reaching forth unto those things which are before, I press toward the mark for the prize of the high calling of God in Christ Jesus. (Philippians 3:13-14)

THE NEED FOR DISCERNMENT

Former Moody Bible Church pastor Dr. Harry Ironside wrote an article regarding the importance of discernment titled "Exposing Error: Is it Worthwhile?" It basically echoes and elaborates on what the apostle Paul stated in Galatians 5:9 and Ephesians 5:10-13—that it is incumbent upon believers to expose and repudiate any error (leaven) that arises in one's life and in the church. Ironside writes:

Error is like leaven, of which we read, "A little leaven leaveneth the whole lump." Truth mixed with error is equivalent to all error, except that it is more innocent looking and therefore, more dangerous. God hates such a mixture! Any error, or any truth-and-error mixture, calls for definite exposure and repudiation. To condone such is to be unfaithful to God and His Word and treacherous to imperiled souls for whom Christ died.[1]

It is not divisive to point out error. We are told in Romans 16:17 to "mark them which cause divisions and offences contrary to the doctrine which ye have learned." It is a mandate to be watchful and discerning and to expose error when it is in our midst.

CONCLUSION

Without a watchful and discerning heart, we are too easily deceived by a crafty adversary. While we rejoice, praise God, give thanks, and remain hopeful through it all, we must be alert to the deception that is all around us. Jesus said—"Take heed that no man deceive you." Be watchful. Be discerning. Keep looking up. Keep pressing on.

CHAPTER FOUR

GOD'S HELP AND COMFORT
THROUGH IT ALL

I will lift up mine eyes unto the hills, from whence cometh my help. My help cometh from the LORD, which made heaven and earth. (Psalm 121:1-2)

For the Lord GOD will help me; therefore shall I not be confounded: therefore have I set my face like a flint, and I know that I shall not be ashamed. (Isaiah 50:7)

For I the LORD thy God will hold thy right hand, saying unto thee, Fear not; I will help thee. (Isaiah 41:13)

Henry Francis Lyte completed the lyrics of his hymn *Abide With Me* shortly before his passing in 1847. Aware that death was near, he directed his hymn to God who he described as the "Help of the helpless."

> Abide with me! Fast falls the eventide;
> The darkness deepens; Lord with me abide.
> When other helpers fail and comforts flee,
> Help of the helpless, O abide with me!

The 1719 hymn *O God, Our Help in Ages Past* by Isaac Watts and William Croft, reminds us that God has been our help in the past and will continue to be our hope in the years to come:

> O God, our help in ages past,
> Our hope for years to come;
> Be Thou our guide while life shall
> last, And our eternal home.

The following Scriptures refer directly to the help and comfort God brings to those who put their faith and trust in Him:

GOD'S HELP

GOD IS OUR HELPER

Behold, God is mine helper. (Psalm 54:4)

So that we may boldly say, The Lord is my helper, and I will not fear what man shall do unto me. (Hebrews 13:6)

GOD HELPS US

Fear thou not; for I am with thee: be not dismayed; for I am thy God: I will strengthen thee; yea, I will help thee; yea, I will uphold thee with the right hand of my righteousness. (Isaiah 41:10)

For the Lord GOD will help me; therefore shall I not be confounded: therefore have I set my face like a flint, and I know that I shall not be ashamed. (Isaiah 50:7)

GOD IS OUR HELP AND OUR SHIELD

Our soul waiteth for the LORD: he is our help and our shield. (Psalm 33:20)

The LORD is my strength and my shield; my heart trusted in him, and I am helped: therefore my heart greatly rejoiceth; and with my song will I praise him. (Psalm 28:7)

GOD IS OUR HELP AND OUR DELIVERER

But I am poor and needy; yet the Lord thinketh upon me: thou art my help and my deliverer; make no tarrying, O my God. (Psalm 40:17)

But I am poor and needy: make haste unto me, O God: thou art my help and my deliverer; O LORD, make no tarrying. (Psalm 70:5)

GOD HELPS DELIVER US FROM THE WICKED

And the LORD shall help them, and deliver them: he shall deliver them from the wicked, and save them, because they trust in him. (Psalm 37:40)

Who will rise up for me against the evildoers? or who will stand up for me against the workers of iniquity? Unless the LORD had been my help, my soul had almost dwelt in silence. (Psalm 94:16-17)

WE PRAY TO GOD FOR HELP

Give us help from trouble: for vain is the help of man. (Psalm 108:12)

Help me, O LORD my God: O save me according to thy mercy: That they may know that this is thy hand; that thou, LORD, hast done it. (Psalm 109:26-27)

Help, LORD; for the godly man ceaseth; for the faithful fail from among the children of men. (Psalm 12:1)

O God, be not far from me: O my God, make haste for my help. (Psalm 71:12)

Forsake me not, O LORD: O my God, be not far from me. Make haste to help me, O Lord my salvation. (Psalm 38:21-22)

Be pleased, O LORD, to deliver me: O LORD, make haste to help me. (Psalm 40:13)

Deliver me from the workers of iniquity, and save me from bloody men. For, lo, they lie in wait for my soul: the mighty are gathered against me; not for my transgression, nor for my sin, O LORD. They run and prepare themselves without my fault: awake to help me, and behold. (Psalm 59:2-4)

GOD IS OUR HELP IN TIMES OF TROUBLE

God is our refuge and strength, a very present help in trouble. (Psalm 46:1)

Let us therefore come boldly unto the throne of grace, that we may obtain mercy, and find grace to help in time of need. (Hebrews 4:16)

Give us help from trouble: for vain is the help of man. (Psalm 60:11)

Gracious is the LORD, and righteous; yea, our God is merciful. The LORD preserveth the simple: I was brought low, and he helped me. (Psalm 116:5-6)

WE REJOICE IN GOD'S HELP

Because thou hast been my help, therefore in the shadow of thy wings will I rejoice. (Psalm 63:7)

GOD HELPS WITH OUR INFIRMITIES

Likewise the Spirit also helpeth our infirmities: for we know not what we should pray for as we ought: but the Spirit itself maketh intercession for us with groanings which cannot be uttered. (Romans 8:26)

OUR HELP IS IN THE NAME OF THE LORD

Blessed be the LORD, who hath not given us as a prey to their teeth. Our soul is escaped as a bird out of the snare of the fowlers: the snare is broken, and we are escaped. Our help is in the name of the LORD, who made heaven and earth. (Psalm 124:6-8)

GOD'S COMFORT

GOD IS THE GOD OF ALL COMFORT

Blessed be God, even the Father of our Lord Jesus Christ, the Father of mercies, and the God of all comfort. (2 Corinthians 1:3)

GOD COMFORTS HIS PEOPLE

I, even I, am he that comforteth you: who art thou, that thou shouldest be afraid of a man that shall die, and of the son of man which shall be made as grass. (Isaiah 51:12)

Sing, O heavens; and be joyful, O earth; and break forth into singing, O mountains: for the LORD hath comforted his people, and will have mercy upon his afflicted. (Isaiah 49:13)

GOD'S HOLY SPIRIT IS OUR COMFORTER

But the Comforter, which is the Holy Ghost, whom the Father will send in my name, he shall teach you all things, and bring all things to your remembrance, whatsoever I have said unto you. (John 14:26)

GOD'S HOLY SPIRIT ABIDES WITH BELIEVERS FOREVER

And I will pray the Father, and he shall give you another Comforter, that he may abide with you for ever; Even the Spirit of truth; whom the world cannot receive, because it seeth him not, neither knoweth him: but ye know him; for he dwelleth with you, and shall be in you. (John 14:16-17)

GOD COMFORTS WITH HIS WORD

For whatsoever things were written aforetime were written for our learning, that we through patience and comfort of the scriptures might have hope. (Romans 15:4)

GOD COMFORTS THOSE WHO ARE CAST DOWN

Nevertheless God, that comforteth those that are cast down, comforted us by the coming of Titus. (2 Corinthians 7:6)

GOD COMFORTS IN OUR TRIBULATION

Who comforteth us in all our tribulation, that we may be able to comfort them which are in any trouble, by the comfort wherewith we ourselves are comforted of God. (2 Corinthians 1:4)

GOD COMFORTS IN TIMES OF DESPAIR

Yea, though I walk through the valley of the shadow of death, I will fear no evil: for thou art with me; thy rod and thy staff they comfort me. (Psalm 23:4)

GOD COMFORTS ON EVERY SIDE

Thy righteousness also, O God, is very high, who hast done great things: O God, who is like unto thee! Thou, which hast showed me great and sore troubles, shalt quicken me again, and shalt bring me up again from the depths of the earth. Thou shalt increase my greatness, and comfort me on every side. (Psalm 71:19-21)

GOD COMFORTS THOSE WHO MOURN

The spirit of the Lord GOD is upon me; because the LORD hath anointed me to preach good tidings unto the meek; he hath sent me to bind up the brokenhearted, to proclaim liberty to the captives, and the opening of the prison to them that are bound . . . to comfort all that mourn. (Isaiah 61:1-2)

Blessed are they that mourn: for they shall be comforted. (Matthew 5:4)

GOD'S COMFORT CAN BE MATERNAL

For thus saith the LORD, Behold, I will extend peace to her like a river, and the glory of the Gentiles like a flowing stream: then shall ye suck, ye shall be borne upon her sides, and be dandled upon her knees. As one whom his mother comforteth, so will I comfort you; and ye shall be comforted in Jerusalem. (Isaiah 66:12-13)

GOD COMFORTS US WITH THE PROMISE OF HIS RETURN

. . . we which are alive and remain unto the coming of the Lord shall not prevent them which are asleep. For the Lord himself shall descend from heaven with a shout, with the voice of the archangel, and with the trump of God: and the dead in Christ shall rise first: Then we which are alive and remain shall be caught up together with them in the clouds, to meet the Lord in the air: and so shall we ever be with the Lord. Wherefore comfort one another with these words. (1 Thessalonians 4:15-18)

SOME HELPFUL AND COMFORTING VERSES

THE LORD IS AROUND HIS PEOPLE

As the mountains are round about Jerusalem, so the LORD is round about his people from henceforth even for ever. (Psalm 25:2)

HE GOES BEFORE US

Be strong and of a good courage, fear not, nor be afraid of them: for the LORD thy God, he it is that doth go with thee; he will not fail thee, nor forsake thee. (Deuteronomy 31:6)

HE NEVER LEAVES US OR FORSAKES US

Let your conversation be without covetousness; and be content with such things as ye have: for he hath said, I will never leave thee, nor forsake thee. (Hebrews 13:5)

NOTHING CAN SEPARATE US FROM THE LOVE OF GOD

Who shall separate us from the love of Christ? shall tribulation, or distress, or persecution, or famine, or nakedness, or peril, or sword? As it is written, For thy sake we are killed all the day long; we are accounted as sheep for the slaughter. Nay, in all these things we are more than conquerors through him that loved us. For I am persuaded, that neither death, nor life, nor angels, nor principalities, nor powers, nor things present, nor things to come, Nor height, nor depth, nor any other creature, shall be able to separate us from the love of God, which is in Christ Jesus our Lord. (Romans 8:35-39)

HE HAS GIVEN US HIS WORD

All scripture is given by inspiration of God, and is profitable for doctrine, for reproof, for correction, for instruction in righteousness: That the man of God may be perfect, thoroughly furnished unto all good works. (2 Timothy 3:16-17)

HIS WORD IS QUICK AND POWERFUL

For the word of God is quick, and powerful, and sharper than any twoedged sword, piercing even to the dividing asunder of soul and spirit, and of the joints and marrow, and is a discerner of the thoughts and intents of the heart. (Hebrews 4:12)

HIS WORD NEVER PASSES AWAY

Heaven and earth shall pass away, but my words shall not pass away. (Matthew 24:35)

HE GIVES US WISDOM

If any of you lack wisdom, let him ask of God, that giveth to all men liberally, and upbraideth not; and it shall be given him. (James 1:5)

HE WILL GUIDE US CONTINUALLY

And the LORD shall guide thee continually, and satisfy thy soul in drought, and make fat thy bones: and thou shalt be like a watered garden, and like a spring of water, whose waters fail not. (Isaiah 58:11)

HE WILL DIRECT OUR PATHS

Trust in the LORD with all thine heart; and lean not unto thine own understanding. In all thy ways acknowledge him, and he shall direct thy paths. (Proverbs 3:5-6)

HE SUPPLIES ALL OUR NEEDS

But my God shall supply all your need according to his riches in glory by Christ Jesus. (Philippians 4:19)

THE LORD'S COMPASSION NEVER FAILS

It is of the LORD'S mercies that we are not consumed, because his compassions fail not. They are new every morning: great is thy faithfulness. (Lamentations 3:22-23)

HE GIVES STRENGTH TO THE WEARY

Hast thou not known? hast thou not heard, that the everlasting God, the LORD, the Creator of the ends of the earth, fainteth not, neither is weary? there is no searching of his understanding. He giveth power to the faint; and to them that have no might he increaseth strength. Even the youths shall faint and be weary, and the young men shall utterly fall: But they that wait upon the LORD shall renew their strength; they shall mount up with wings as eagles; they shall run, and not be weary; and they shall walk, and not faint. (Isaiah 40:28-31)

HE GIVES US HIS PEACE

Peace I leave with you, my peace I give unto you: not as the world giveth, give I unto you. Let not your heart be troubled, neither let it be afraid. (John 14:27)

HE KEEPS US IN HIS PEACE

Thou wilt keep him in perfect peace, whose mind is stayed on thee: because he trusteth in thee. (Isaiah 26:3)

HIS PEACE KEEPS OUR HEARTS AND MINDS

Be careful for nothing; but in every thing by prayer and supplication with thanksgiving let your requests be made known unto God. And the peace of God, which passeth all understanding, shall keep your hearts and minds through Christ Jesus. (Philippians 4:6-7)

HE IS OUR REFUGE

The LORD also will be a refuge for the oppressed, a refuge in times of trouble. (Psalm 9:9)

HE DELIVERS US FROM AFFLICTION

Many are the afflictions of the righteous: but the LORD delivereth him out of them all. (Psalm 34:19)

HE GIVES US REST

Come unto me, all ye that labour and are heavy laden, and I will give you rest. Take my yoke upon you, and learn of me; for I am meek and lowly in heart: and ye shall find rest unto your souls. For my yoke is easy, and my burden is light. (Matthew 11:28-30)

HE PERFECTS HIS STRENGTH IN OUR WEAKNESS

And he said unto me, My grace is sufficient for thee: for my strength is made perfect in weakness. (2 Corinthians 12:9)

WE CAN DO ALL THINGS THROUGH CHRIST WHO STRENGTHENS US

I can do all things through Christ which strengtheneth me. (Philippians 4:13)

HE WORKS ALL THINGS FOR GOOD FOR THOSE WHO LOVE HIM

And we know that all things work together for good to them that love God, to them who are the called according to his purpose. (Romans 8:28)

HE IS ABLE TO KEEP US FROM FALLING

Now unto him that is able to keep you from falling, and to present you faultless before the presence of his glory with exceeding joy. (Jude 1:24)

HE PROTECTS US

When thou passest through the waters, I will be with thee; and through the rivers, they shall not overflow thee: when thou walkest through the fire, thou shalt not be burned; neither shall the flame kindle upon thee. (Isaiah 43:2)

HE LIFTS UP A STANDARD AGAINST THE ENEMY

When the enemy shall come in like a flood, the Spirit of the LORD shall lift up a standard against him. (Isaiah 59:19)

NO WEAPON SHALL PROSPER AGAINST US

No weapon that is formed against thee shall prosper. (Isaiah 54:17)

HE GIVES US THE VICTORY THROUGH JESUS CHRIST

But thanks be to God, which giveth us the victory through our Lord Jesus Christ. (1 Corinthians 15:57)

HE IS FAITHFUL TO COMPLETE HIS WORK IN US

Being confident of this very thing, that he which hath begun a good work in you will perform it until the day of Jesus Christ. (Philippians 1:6)

HE IS OUR GUIDE UNTO DEATH

For this God is our God for ever and ever: he will be our guide even unto death. (Psalm 48:14)

HE GIVES US ETERNAL LIFE

For God so loved the world, that he gave his only begotten Son, that whosoever believeth in him should not perish, but have everlasting life. (John 3:16)

ETERNAL LIFE IS A GIFT FROM GOD

For the wages of sin is death; but the gift of God is eternal life through Jesus Christ our Lord. (Romans 6:23)

GOD SENT HIS SON TO BE THE PROPITIATION FOR OUR SINS

Herein is love, not that we loved God, but that he loved us, and sent his Son to be the propitiation for our sins. (1 John 4:10)

IF WE CONFESS OUR SINS HE FORGIVES US

If we confess our sins, he is faithful and just to forgive us our sins, and to cleanse us from all unrighteousness. (1 John 1:9)

WHOEVER CALLS UPON THE LORD'S NAME SHALL BE SAVED

For whosoever shall call upon the name of the Lord shall be saved. (Romans 10:13)

BY GRACE WE ARE SAVED THROUGH FAITH

For by grace are ye saved through faith; and that not of yourselves: it is the gift of God: Not of works, lest any man should boast. (Ephesians 2:8-9)

HE HAS PREPARED A PLACE FOR US

Let not your heart be troubled: ye believe in God, believe also in me. In my Father's house are many mansions: if it were not so, I would have told you. I go to prepare a place for you. And if I go and prepare a place for you, I will come again, and receive you unto myself; that where I am, there ye may be also. (John 14:1-3)

HE WILL RAISE US UP

Knowing that he which raised up the Lord Jesus shall raise up us also by Jesus, and shall present us with you. (2 Corinthians 4:14)

HIS GLORY WILL BE REVEALED IN US

For I reckon that the sufferings of this present time are not worthy to be compared with the glory which shall be revealed in us. (Romans 8:18)

HE WILL WIPE AWAY ALL TEARS

And God shall wipe away all tears from their eyes; and there shall be no more death, neither sorrow, nor crying, neither shall there be any more pain: for the former things are passed away. (Revelation 21:4)

WHAT GOD HAS PREPARED FOR THOSE WHO LOVE HIM

But as it is written, Eye hath not seen, nor ear heard, neither have entered into the heart of man, the things which God hath prepared for them that love him. (1 Corinthians 2:9)

OUR HELPER AND OUR COMFORTER

Lines from the following two hymns echo what the Bible makes very clear. God is our rock, our hiding place, our refuge and defense—our helper ever near. He is our shelter in the time of storm, our wonderful Savior and comfort sweet. In good times and in bad, He is our Helper and our Comforter through it all.

SHELTER IN THE TIME OF STORM

The Lord's our Rock, in Him we hide,
A Shelter in the time of storm;
Secure whatever ill betide,
A Shelter in the time of storm.
A shade by day, defense by night,
A Shelter in the time of storm;
No fears alarm, no foes afright,
A Shelter in the time of storm.

The raging storms may round us beat,
A Shelter in the time of storm;
We'll never leave our safe Retreat,
A Shelter in the time of storm.

O Rock divine, O Refuge dear,
A Shelter in the time of storm;
Be thou our helper ever near,
A Shelter in the time of storm.

—Vernon J. Charlesworth (1878)

NEAR TO THE HEART OF GOD

There is a place of comfort sweet,
Near to the heart of God,
A place where we our Savior meet,
Near to the heart of God.

—Cleland B. McAfee (1903)

CHAPTER FIVE

BEING THANKFUL THROUGH IT ALL

In every thing give thanks: for this is the will of God in Christ Jesus concerning you. (1 Thessalonians 5:18)

Thankfulness is our attempt as believers to express the inexpressible—the amazing gratitude we feel for the amazing grace bestowed upon us by our Lord and Savior Jesus Christ. He not only saved us from our sins (1 John 2:2), He promised to never leave us or forsake us (Hebrews 13:5). We are also assured that He who began "a good work" in us will be faithful to "perform it until the day of Jesus Christ" (Philippians 1:6).

A day for Thanksgiving was set aside as a holiday so that we, as a nation, could collectively give thanks to God for all of His blessings—to express our gratitude for His love and protection and provision. In years past, hymns like *Come Ye Thankful People Come* were commonly sung in churches and classrooms as Thanksgiving day approached—young and old alike openly giving thanks to God for His abundant supply and bounty:

Come, ye thankful people come;
Raise the song of harvest home,

All is safely gathered in,
Ere the winter storms begin.
God, our Maker, doth provide,
For our wants to be supplied;
Come to God's own temple come;
Raise the song of harvest home.

God's people are called to be a thankful people because we have so much to be thankful for. Another hymn of gratitude, *Now Thank We All Our God,* expresses our thanks for all the "wondrous things" God has done and for His "countless gifts of love":

Now thank we all our God,
With hearts and hands and voices,
Who, wondrous things hath done,
In whom this world rejoices;
Who, from our mothers' arms,
Hath blessed us on our way,
With countless gifts of love,
And still is ours today.

—Martin Ringkart (1636)

135 REFERENCES IN THE KJV BIBLE

In the *King James Bible,* for example, there are 135 separate verses that refer to the act of giving thanks. Scripture makes it clear that thankfulness is pleasing to God and is part of the way we praise and worship Him (Psalm 116:12-19). We should never take things for granted because we know that "every good gift and every perfect gift is from above" (James 1:17).

Jesus stressed the importance of thankfulness when He singled out the only one of the ten healed lepers who glorified God and gave thanks for his healing:

And one of them, when he saw that he was healed, turned back, and with a loud voice glorified God, And fell down on his face at his feet, giving him thanks: and he was a Samaritan. And Jesus answering said, Were there not ten cleansed? but where are the nine? There are not found that returned to give glory to God, save this stranger. And he said unto him, Arise, go thy way: thy faith hath made thee whole. (Luke 17:15-19)

Jonah was released from the fish's belly after praying and giving thanks to the Lord:

When my soul fainted within me I remembered the LORD: and my prayer came in unto thee, into thine holy temple. They that observe lying vanities forsake their own mercy. But I will sacrifice unto thee with the voice of thanksgiving; I will pay that I have vowed. Salvation is of the LORD. And the LORD spake unto the fish, and it vomited out Jonah upon the dry land. (Jonah 2:7-10)

King David, though continually attacked by his enemies, was always thanking God for His goodness and mercy and deliverance:

He delivereth me from mine enemies: yea, thou liftest me up above those that rise up against me: thou hast delivered me from the violent man. Therefore will I give thanks unto thee, O LORD, among the heathen, and sing praises unto thy name. Great deliverance giveth he to his king; and showeth mercy to his anointed, to David, and to his seed for evermore. (Psalm 18:48-50)

Daniel's response to the King Darius' edict forbidding prayer to anyone other than the King was to continue his practice of openly praying and giving thanks to his God. Scripture records that Daniel was delivered from certain death in the lion's den because he unashamedly "believed in his God" (Daniel 6:10;23). His refusal to compromise served as a witness not only to the King but to all those who have read this account in the Bible:

> Wherefore king Darius signed the writing and the decree. Now when Daniel knew that the writing was signed, he went into his house; and his windows being open in his chamber toward Jerusalem, he kneeled upon his knees three times a day, and prayed, and gave thanks before his God, as he did aforetime. (Daniel 6:9-10)

> Then was the king exceeding glad for him, and commanded that they should take Daniel up out of the den. So Daniel was taken up out of the den, and no manner of hurt was found upon him, because he believed in his God. (Daniel 6:23)

As already referenced, Scripture is replete with verses pertaining to giving thanks to God for His abiding presence in our lives. Much too frequently we neglect to give thanks to the One True God to Whom we have so much to be grateful for. The Bible is very specific about the many whys and wherefores of giving thanks to God.

WHY WE GIVE THANKS

BECAUSE GOD GIVES US OUR DAILY BREAD

> Now he that ministereth seed to the sower both minister bread for your food, and multiply your seed sown, and increase the fruits of your righteousness; Being enriched in every thing to all bountifulness, which causeth through us thanksgiving to God. For the administration of this service not only supplieth the want of the saints, but is abundant also by many thanksgivings unto God. (2 Corinthians 9:10-12)

> And he took the seven loaves and the fishes, and gave thanks, and brake them, and gave to his disciples, and the disciples to the multitude. And they did all eat, and were filled: and they took up of the broken meat that was left seven baskets full. And

they that did eat were four thousand men, beside women and children. (Matthew 15:36-38)

For every creature of God is good, and nothing to be refused, if it be received with thanksgiving: For it is sanctified by the word of God and prayer. (1 Timothy 4:4-5)

BECAUSE GOD IS GOOD

O give thanks unto the LORD; for he is good; for his mercy endureth for ever. (1 Chronicles 16:34)

And they sang together by course in praising and giving thanks unto the LORD; because he is good, for his mercy endureth for ever toward Israel. (Ezra 3:11)

BECAUSE THANKFULNESS IS GOOD

It is a good thing to give thanks unto the LORD, and to sing praises unto thy name, O most High. (Psalm 92:1)

BECAUSE THANKFULNESS IS THE WILL OF GOD

In every thing give thanks: for this is the will of God in Christ Jesus concerning you. (1 Thessalonians 5:18)

BECAUSE GOD IS HOLY

Sing unto the LORD, O ye saints of his, and give thanks at the remembrance of his holiness. (Psalm 30:4)

Rejoice in the LORD, ye righteous; and give thanks at the remembrance of his holiness. (Psalm 97:12)

BECAUSE GOD'S NAME IS HOLY

Save us, O LORD our God, and gather us from among the heathen, to give thanks unto thy holy name, and to triumph in thy praise. (Psalm 106:47)

And say ye, Save us, O God of our salvation, and gather us together, and deliver us from the heathen, that we may give thanks to thy holy name, and glory in thy praise. (1 Chronicles 16:35)

BECAUSE GOD'S WORD IS HOLY

For this cause also thank we God without ceasing, because, when ye received the word of God which ye heard of us, ye received it not as the word of men, but as it is in truth, the word of God, which effectually worketh also in you that believe. (1 Thessalonians 2:13)

And that from a child thou hast known the holy scriptures, which are able to make thee wise unto salvation through faith which is in Christ Jesus. All scripture is given by inspiration of God, and is profitable for doctrine, for reproof, for correction, for instruction in righteousness: That the man of God may be perfect, thoroughly furnished unto all good works. (2 Timothy 3:15-17)

BECAUSE OF GOD'S GRACE

Knowing that he which raised up the Lord Jesus shall raise up us also by Jesus, and shall present us with you. For all things are for your sakes, that the abundant grace might through the thanksgiving of many redound to the glory of God. (2 Corinthians 4:14-15)

BECAUSE GOD GAVE US THE GIFT OF JESUS CHRIST

Thanks be unto God for his unspeakable gift. (2 Corinthians 9:15)

BECAUSE JESUS CHRIST SHED HIS BLOOD FOR OUR SINS

And as they were eating, Jesus took bread, and blessed it, and brake it, and gave it to the disciples, and said, Take, eat; this is my body. And he took the cup, and gave thanks, and gave it to them, saying, Drink ye all of it; For this is my blood of the new testament, which is shed for many for the remission of sins. (Matthew 26:26-28)

BECAUSE GOD LIFTS US ABOVE OUR ENEMIES

It is God that avengeth me, and that bringeth down the people under me, And that bringeth me forth from mine enemies: thou also hast lifted me up on high above them that rose up against me: thou hast delivered me from the violent man. Therefore I will give thanks unto thee, O LORD, among the heathen, and I will sing praises unto thy name. (2 Samuel 22:48-50)

He delivereth me from mine enemies: yea, thou liftest me up above those that rise up against me: thou hast delivered me from the violent man. Therefore will I give thanks unto thee, O LORD, among the heathen, and sing praises unto thy name. (Psalm 18:48-49)

BECAUSE GOD DELIVERED US FROM THE POWERS OF DARKNESS

That ye might walk worthy of the Lord unto all pleasing, being fruitful in every good work, and increasing in the knowledge of God; Strengthened with all might, according to his glorious power, unto all patience and longsuffering with joyfulness; Giving thanks unto the Father, which hath made us meet to be partakers of the inheritance of the saints in light: Who hath delivered us from the power of darkness, and hath translated us into the kingdom of his dear Son: In whom we have redemption through his blood, even the forgiveness of sins. (Colossians 1:10-14)

BECAUSE GOD CAUSES US TO TRIUMPH IN CHRIST

Now thanks be unto God, which always causeth us to triumph in Christ, and maketh manifest the savour of his knowledge by us in every place. (2 Corinthians 2:14)

BECAUSE GOD GIVES US THE VICTORY THROUGH JESUS CHRIST

O death, where is thy sting? O grave, where is thy victory? The sting of death is sin; and the strength of sin is the law. But thanks be to God, which giveth us the victory through our Lord Jesus Christ. Therefore, my beloved brethren, be ye stedfast, unmoveable, always abounding in the work of the Lord, forasmuch as ye know that your labour is not in vain in the Lord. (1 Corinthians 15:55-58)

BECAUSE GOD'S MERCY ENDURES FOREVER

Praise ye the LORD. O give thanks unto the LORD; for he is good: for his mercy endureth for ever. (Psalm 106:1)

O give thanks unto the God of gods: for his mercy endureth for ever. (Psalm 136:2)

O give thanks to the Lord of lords: for his mercy endureth for ever. (Psalm 136:3)

O give thanks unto the God of heaven: for his mercy endureth for ever. (Psalm 136:26)

HOW WE GIVE THANKS

THROUGH JESUS CHRIST

First, I thank my God through Jesus Christ for you all, that your faith is spoken of throughout the whole world. (Romans 1:8)

For there is one God, and one mediator between God and men, the man Christ Jesus; Who gave himself a ransom for all, to be testified in due time. (1 Timothy 2:5-6)

WITH THE SACRIFICE OF THANKSGIVING

Oh that men would praise the LORD for his goodness, and for his wonderful works to the children of men! And let them sacrifice the sacrifices of thanksgiving, and declare his works with rejoicing. (Psalm 107:21-22)

I will offer to thee the sacrifice of thanksgiving, and will call upon the name of the LORD. (Psalm 116:17)

BY PRAISING AND GIVING THANKS TO HIS NAME

Let us go forth therefore unto him without the camp, bearing his reproach. For here have we no continuing city, but we seek one to come. By him therefore let us offer the sacrifice of praise to God continually, that is, the fruit of our lips giving thanks to his name. But to do good and to communicate forget not: for with such sacrifices God is well pleased. (Hebrews 13:13-16)

THROUGH PRAYER

Be careful for nothing; but in every thing by prayer and supplication with thanksgiving let your requests be made known unto God. And the peace of God, which passeth all understanding, shall keep your hearts and minds through Christ Jesus. (Philippians 4:6-7)

Continue in prayer, and watch in the same with thanksgiving. (Colossians 4:2)

THROUGH SONG

Sing unto the LORD with thanksgiving; sing praise upon the harp unto our God. (Psalm 147:7)

I will praise the name of God with a song, and will magnify him with thanksgiving. (Psalm 69:30)

It came even to pass, as the trumpeters and singers were as one, to make one sound to be heard in praising and thanking the LORD. (2 Chronicles 5:13)

O come, let us sing unto the LORD: let us make a joyful noise to the rock of our salvation. Let us come before his presence with thanksgiving, and make a joyful noise unto him with psalms. For the LORD is a great God, and a great King above all gods. (Psalm 95:1-3)

BY WALKING IN LOVE AND THANKFULNESS

Be ye therefore followers of God, as dear children; And walk in love, as Christ also hath loved us, and hath given himself for us an offering and a sacrifice to God for a sweetsmelling savour. But fornication, and all uncleanness, or covetousness, let it not be once named among you, as becometh saints; Neither filthiness, nor foolish talking, nor jesting, which are not convenient: but rather giving of thanks. (Ephesians 5:1-4)

BY DECLARING HIS WORKS

That I may publish with the voice of thanksgiving, and tell of all thy wondrous works. (Psalm 26:7)

Give thanks unto the LORD, call upon his name, make known his deeds among the people. Sing unto him, sing psalms unto him, talk ye of all his wondrous works. (1 Chronicles 16:8-9)

BY THANKING GOD FOR FELLOW BELIEVERS

Paul, an apostle of Jesus Christ by the will of God, and Timotheus our brother, To the saints and faithful brethren in Christ which are at Colosse: Grace be unto you, and peace, from God our Father and the Lord Jesus Christ. We give thanks to God and the Father of our Lord Jesus Christ, praying always for you. (Colossians 1:1-3)

But we are bound to give thanks alway to God for you, brethren beloved of the Lord, because God hath from the beginning chosen you to salvation through sanctification of the Spirit and belief of the truth: Whereunto he called you by our gospel, to the obtaining of the glory of our Lord Jesus Christ. Therefore, brethren, stand fast, and hold the traditions which ye have been taught, whether by word, or our epistle. (2 Thessalonians 2:13-15)

BY THANKING GOD FOR ALL MEN

I exhort therefore, that, first of all, supplications, prayers, intercessions, and giving of thanks, be made for all men; For kings, and for all that are in authority; that we may lead a quiet and peaceable life in all godliness and honesty. For this is good and acceptable in the sight of God our Saviour; Who will have all men to be saved, and to come unto the knowledge of the truth. (1 Timothy 2:1-4)

BY GIVING THANKS IN EVERYTHING

In every thing give thanks: for this is the will of God in Christ Jesus concerning you. (1 Thessalonians 5:18)

BY GIVING THANKS IN WHATEVER WE DO

And let the peace of God rule in your hearts, to the which also ye are called in one body; and be ye thankful. Let the word of Christ dwell in you richly in all wisdom; teaching and admonishing one another in psalms and hymns and spiritual songs, singing with grace in your hearts to the Lord. And whatsoever ye do in word or deed, do all in the name of the Lord Jesus, giving thanks to God and the Father by him. (Colossians 3:15-17)

As ye have therefore received Christ Jesus the Lord, so walk ye in him: Rooted and built up in him, and stablished in the faith, as ye have been taught, abounding therein with thanksgiving. (Colossians 2:6-7)

WHO GIVES THANKS

THE ANGELS

And all the angels stood round about the throne, and about the elders and the four beasts, and fell before the throne on their faces, and worshipped God, Saying, Amen: Blessing, and glory, and wisdom, and thanksgiving, and honour, and power, and might, be unto our God for ever and ever. Amen. (Revelation 7:11-12)

THE 24 ELDERS IN HEAVEN

And the four and twenty elders, which sat before God on their seats, fell upon their faces, and worshipped God, Saying, We give thee thanks, O Lord God Almighty, which art, and wast, and art to come; because thou hast taken to thee thy great power, and hast reigned. (Revelation 11:16-17)

ALL HIS PEOPLE

Make a joyful noise unto the LORD, all ye lands. Serve the LORD with gladness: come before his presence with singing. Know ye that the LORD he is God: it is he that hath made us, and not we ourselves; we are his people, and the sheep of his pasture. Enter into his gates with thanksgiving, and into his courts with praise: be thankful unto him, and bless his name. For the LORD is good; his mercy is everlasting; and his truth endureth to all generations. (Psalm 100:1-5)

WHEN WE GIVE THANKS

WHEN WE EAT OR DON'T EAT

He that regardeth the day, regardeth it unto the Lord; and he that regardeth not the day, to the Lord he doth not regard it. He that eateth, eateth to the Lord, for he giveth God thanks;

and he that eateth not, to the Lord he eateth not, and giveth God thanks. (Romans 14:6)

WHEN WE TAKE COMMUNION

And he took the cup, and gave thanks, and said, Take this, and divide it among yourselves: For I say unto you, I will not drink of the fruit of the vine, until the kingdom of God shall come. And he took bread, and gave thanks, and brake it, and gave unto them, saying, This is my body which is given for you: this do in remembrance of me. (Luke 22:17-19)

WHEN WE HAVE SUFFERED WRONGFULLY

For this is thankworthy, if a man for conscience toward God endure grief, suffering wrongfully. For what glory is it, if, when ye be buffeted for your faults, ye shall take it patiently? but if, when ye do well, and suffer for it, ye take it patiently, this is acceptable with God. (1 Peter 2:19-20)

BEFORE TROUBLE

Offer unto God thanksgiving; and pay thy vows unto the most High: And call upon me in the day of trouble: I will deliver thee, and thou shalt glorify me. (Psalm 50:14-15)

AFTER GOD INTERVENES

And one of them, when he saw that he was healed, turned back, and with a loud voice glorified God, And fell down on his face at his feet, giving him thanks: and he was a Samaritan. (Luke 17:15-16)

MORNING AND EVENING

And to stand every morning to thank and praise the LORD, and likewise at even. (1 Chronicles 23:30)

AT MIDNIGHT

At midnight I will rise to give thanks unto thee because of thy righteous judgments. (Psalm 119:62)

WHILE WE LIVE

For in death there is no remembrance of thee: in the grave who shall give thee thanks? (Psalm 6:5)

ALWAYS

And be not drunk with wine, wherein is excess; but be filled with the Spirit; Speaking to yourselves in psalms and hymns and spiritual songs, singing and making melody in your heart to the Lord; Giving thanks always for all things unto God and the Father in the name of our Lord Jesus Christ. (Ephesians 5:18-20)

FOREVER

Hear, O LORD, and have mercy upon me: LORD, be thou my helper. Thou hast turned for me my mourning into dancing: thou hast put off my sackcloth, and girded me with gladness; To the end that my glory may sing praise to thee, and not be silent. O LORD my God, I will give thanks unto thee for ever. (Psalm 30:10-12)

So we thy people and sheep of thy pasture will give thee thanks for ever: we will show forth thy praise to all generations. (Psalm 79:13)

WE PRAISE GOD WITH OUR THANKFULNESS

The Bible says that by offering the sacrifice of praise to God we give thanks to Him (Hebrews 13:13-16). Thus by praising God, we thank Him for his love, protection, presence, and provision. Paul and Silas gave thanks to God by praising Him—even after they were beaten and thrown in the jail (Acts 16:23-25). Pursuant to their thankful praise, the prison walls confining them were shaken. Free to escape, they witnessed to the jailer and his whole household who were all saved and baptized that same day (Acts 16:30-34).

With God's help we can learn to give thanks in everything. There is a saying that wherever you go, there you are. The Bible tells believers that wherever they go, God is there with them. Because God is always with us, He will help us and enable us to do things that we otherwise could not do on our own—like giving thanks in everything (1 Thessalonians 5:18) and thanking Him for all things (Ephesians 5:20).

A PRAYER

Lord, I want to be thankful "in everything" because Scripture tells me that is your will for my life. But I am often unable to be thankful due to forgetfulness, selfishness, and my own shortcomings. May Your Holy Spirit remind me to be thankful in everything, now, always, and for evermore. Please help me to remember that all things work together for good to them who are called according to your purpose. Thank You for all that you have done and will continue to do in my life. In Jesus' Name. Amen.

CHAPTER SIX

REMAINING HOPEFUL
THROUGH IT ALL

T O A BELIEVER, the expression "hope springs eternal" means that our hope is always in Jesus Christ. He is our hope because He gives eternal life to those who put their hope and faith in Him (1 Timothy 1:1; Titus 3:5-7). The old hymn, *O God Our Help in Ages Past*, states it simply and beautifully—Christian hope springs eternal because God is our hope and our eternal home.

> O God our help in ages past,
> Our hope for years to come
> Our shelter from the stormy blast,
> And our eternal home. [1]

Another much revered hymn—*My Hope is Built on Nothing Less*—emphatically states that our hope is founded on nothing less than Jesus' blood and righteousness:

> My hope is built on nothing less
> Than Jesus' blood and righteousness.
> I dare not trust the sweetest frame,
> But wholly lean on Jesus' name. [2]

The modern-day hymn *In Christ Alone* reminds us that it is in Christ Jesus alone that our hope is found:

> In Christ alone my hope is found,
> He is my Light, my strength, my song
> This Cornerstone, this Solid Ground,
> Firm through the fiercest drought and storm.
> What heights of love, what depths of peace,
> When fears are stilled, when strivings cease!
> My comforter, my all in all;
> Here in the love of Christ I stand.[3]

Because our hope is in Him, we look to His Word to strengthen our hope. The Bible is filled with verses on why we hope in the Lord and what we are to do with our hope. What follows are some of these verses.

WHY WE HOPE IN THE LORD

BECAUSE HE IS THE HOPE OF ISRAEL

O LORD, the hope of Israel, all that forsake thee shall be ashamed, and they that depart from me shall be written in the earth, because they have forsaken the LORD, the fountain of living waters. (Jeremiah 17:13)

BECAUSE HE IS THE GOD OF HOPE

Now the God of hope fill you with all joy and peace in believing, that ye may abound in hope, through the power of the Holy Ghost. (Romans 15:13)

BECAUSE HE IS OUR HOPE

Paul, an apostle of Jesus Christ by the commandment of God our Saviour, and Lord Jesus Christ, which is our hope. (1 Timothy 1:1)

Be thou my strong habitation, whereunto I may continually resort: thou hast given commandment to save me; for thou art my rock and my fortress. Deliver me, O my God, out of the hand of the wicked, out of the hand of the unrighteous and cruel man. For thou art my hope, O Lord GOD: thou art my trust from my youth. (Psalm 71:3-5)

And now, Lord, what wait I for? my hope is in thee. (Psalm 39:7)

BECAUSE HE IS THE HOPE OF GLORY

Even the mystery which hath been hid from ages and from generations, but now is made manifest to his saints: To whom God would make known what is the riches of the glory of this mystery among the Gentiles; which is Christ in you, the hope of glory: Whom we preach, warning every man, and teaching every man in all wisdom; that we may present every man perfect in Christ Jesus. (Colossians 1:26-28)

BECAUSE HE IS THE HOPE OF OUR SALVATION

For they that sleep sleep in the night; and they that be drunken are drunken in the night. But let us, who are of the day, be sober, putting on the breastplate of faith and love; and for an helmet, the hope of salvation. For God hath not appointed us to wrath, but to obtain salvation by our Lord Jesus Christ, Who died for us, that, whether we wake or sleep, we should live together with him. Wherefore comfort yourselves together, and edify one another, even as also ye do. (1 Thessalonians 5:7-11)

LORD, I have hoped for thy salvation, and done thy commandments. My soul hath kept thy testimonies; and I love them exceedingly. I have kept thy precepts and thy testimonies: for all my ways are before thee. (Psalm 119:166-168)

BECAUSE OUR HOPE IS IN HIS BLOOD

Forasmuch as ye know that ye were not redeemed with corruptible things, as silver and gold, from your vain conversation received by tradition from your fathers; But with the precious blood of Christ, as of a lamb without blemish and without spot: Who verily was foreordained before the foundation of the world, but was manifest in these last times for you, Who by him do believe in God, that raised him up from the dead, and gave him glory; that your faith and hope might be in God. (1 Peter 1:18-21)

BECAUSE OUR HOPE IS IN HIS RESURRECTION

Blessed be the God and Father of our Lord Jesus Christ, which according to his abundant mercy hath begotten us again unto a lively hope by the resurrection of Jesus Christ from the dead, To an inheritance incorruptible, and undefiled, and that fadeth not away, reserved in heaven for you, Who are kept by the power of God through faith unto salvation ready to be revealed in the last time. (1 Peter 1:3-5)

Who by him do believe in God, that raised him up from the dead, and gave him glory; that your faith and hope might be in God. (1 Peter 1:21)

BECAUSE HE GIVES US HOPE THROUGH HIS GRACE

Now our Lord Jesus Christ himself, and God, even our Father, which hath loved us, and hath given us everlasting consolation and good hope through grace, Comfort your hearts, and stablish you in every good word and work. (2 Thessalonians 2:16-17)

BECAUSE OF OUR HOPE IN HIM, HE HEARS US

For in thee, O LORD, do I hope: thou wilt hear, O Lord my God. (Psalm 38:15)

BECAUSE OUR HOPE IN HIM PURIFIES US

Behold, what manner of love the Father hath bestowed upon us, that we should be called the sons of God: therefore the world knoweth us not, because it knew him not. Beloved, now are we the sons of God, and it doth not yet appear what we shall be: but we know that, when he shall appear, we shall be like him; for we shall see him as he is. And every man that hath this hope in him purifieth himself, even as he is pure. (1 John 3:1-3)

BECAUSE HOPE IN HIM IS OUR ANCHOR

That by two immutable things, in which it was impossible for God to lie, we might have a strong consolation, who have fled for refuge to lay hold upon the hope set before us: Which hope we have as an anchor of the soul, both sure and stedfast, and which entereth into that within the veil; Whither the forerunner is for us entered, even Jesus, made an high priest for ever after the order of Melchisedec. (Hebrews 6:18-20)

BECAUSE OUR HOPE IN HIM PRODUCES FAITH

Now faith is the substance of things hoped for, the evidence of things not seen. (Hebrews 11:1)

BECAUSE WE ARE SAVED BY OUR HOPE IN HIM

For we are saved by hope: but hope that is seen is not hope: for what a man seeth, why doth he yet hope for? But if we hope for that we see not, then do we with patience wait for it. (Romans 8:24-25)

BECAUSE WE ARE BLESSED BY OUR HOPE IN HIM

Blessed is the man that trusteth in the LORD, and whose hope the LORD is. (Jeremiah 17:7)

BECAUSE OUR HOPE IN HIM STRENGTHENS OUR HEART

Be of good courage, and he shall strengthen your heart, all ye that hope in the LORD. (Psalm 31:24)

BECAUSE HE IS THE HOPE AND HEALTH OF OUR COUNTENANCE

Why art thou cast down, O my soul? and why art thou disquieted within me? hope thou in God: for I shall yet praise him, who is the health of my countenance, and my God. (Psalm 42:11)

BECAUSE OUR HOPE IN HIM MAKES US GLAD

The hope of the righteous shall be gladness: but the expectation of the wicked shall perish. (Proverbs 10:28)

BECAUSE OUR HOPE IN HIM MAKES US HAPPY

Happy is he that hath the God of Jacob for his help, whose hope is in the LORD his God. (Psalm 146:5)

BECAUSE OUR HOPE IN HIM DRAWS US NEAR TO GOD

For the law made nothing perfect, but the bringing in of a better hope did; by the which we draw nigh unto God. (Hebrews 7:19)

BECAUSE HE IS OUR HOPE IN THE LAST DAYS

Multitudes, multitudes in the valley of decision: for the day of the LORD is near in the valley of decision. The sun and the moon shall be darkened, and the stars shall withdraw their shining. The LORD also shall roar out of Zion, and utter his voice from Jerusalem; and the heavens and the earth shall shake: but the LORD will be the hope of his people, and the strength of the children of Israel. (Joel 3:14-16)

Be not a terror unto me: thou art my hope in the day of evil. (Jeremiah 17:17)

BECAUSE OF HIM, WE HAVE HOPE IN DEATH

The wicked is driven away in his wickedness: but the righteous hath hope in his death. (Proverbs 14:32)

BECAUSE HE GIVES US THE HOPE OF ETERNAL LIFE

Not by works of righteousness which we have done, but according to his mercy he saved us, by the washing of regeneration, and renewing of the Holy Ghost; Which he shed on us abundantly through Jesus Christ our Saviour; That being justified by his grace, we should be made heirs according to the hope of eternal life. (Titus 3:5-7)

Paul, a servant of God, and an apostle of Jesus Christ, according to the faith of God's elect, and the acknowledging of the truth which is after godliness; In hope of eternal life, which God, that cannot lie, promised before the world began; But hath in due times manifested his word through preaching, which is committed unto me according to the commandment of God our Saviour. (Titus 1:1-3)

Since we heard of your faith in Christ Jesus, and of the love which ye have to all the saints, For the hope which is laid up for you in heaven, whereof ye heard before in the word of the truth of the gospel. (Colossians 1:4-5)

WHAT WE ARE TO DO WITH OUR HOPE

WE ARE TO SET OUR HOPE IN GOD

That they might set their hope in God, and not forget the works of God, but keep his commandments: (Psalm 78:7)

WE ARE TO HOPE IN HIS JUDGEMENTS

And take not the word of truth utterly out of my mouth; for I have hoped in thy judgments. So shall I keep thy law continually for ever and ever. (Psalm 119:43-44)

WE ARE TO HOPE IN HIS WORD

They that fear thee will be glad when they see me; because I have hoped in thy word. (Psalm 119:74)

My soul fainteth for thy salvation: but I hope in thy word. (Psalm 119:81)

I prevented the dawning of the morning, and cried: I hoped in thy word. (Psalm 119:147)

But this I confess unto thee, that after the way which they call heresy, so worship I the God of my fathers, believing all things which are written in the law and in the prophets: And have hope toward God, which they themselves also allow, that there shall be a resurrection of the dead, both of the just and unjust. (Acts 24:14-15)

For whatsoever things were written aforetime were written for our learning, that we through patience and comfort of the scriptures might have hope. (Romans 15:4)

Thou art my hiding place and my shield: I hope in thy word. (Psalm 119:114)

I wait for the LORD, my soul doth wait, and in his word do I hope. (Psalm 130:5)

WE ARE TO HOPE IN HIS MERCY

Behold, the eye of the LORD is upon them that fear him, upon them that hope in his mercy; To deliver their soul from death, and to keep them alive in famine. (Psalm 33:18-19)

The LORD taketh pleasure in them that fear him, in those that hope in his mercy. (Psalm 147:11)

It is of the LORD'S mercies that we are not consumed, because his compassions fail not. They are new every morning: great is thy faithfulness. The LORD is my portion, saith my soul;

therefore will I hope in him. The LORD is good unto them that wait for him, to the soul that seeketh him. It is good that a man should both hope and quietly wait for the salvation of the LORD. (Lamentations 3:22-26)

WE ARE TO HOPE AND WAIT QUIETLY FOR HIS SALVATION

It is good that a man should both hope and quietly wait for the salvation of the LORD. (Lamentations 3:26)

WE ARE TO PLOW AND THRESH WITH HOPE

Or saith he it altogether for our sakes? For our sakes, no doubt, this is written: that he that ploweth should plow in hope; and that he that thresheth in hope should be partaker of his hope. (1 Corinthians 9:10)

WE ARE TO HOPE IN ALL THINGS WITH LOVE AND CHARITY

Charity suffereth long, and is kind; charity envieth not; charity vaunteth not itself, is not puffed up, Doth not behave itself unseemly, seeketh not her own, is not easily provoked, thinketh no evil; Rejoiceth not in iniquity, but rejoiceth in the truth; Beareth all things, believeth all things, hopeth all things, endureth all things. (1 Corinthians 13:4-7)

WE ARE TO REJOICE IN OUR HOPE

Therefore being justified by faith, we have peace with God through our Lord Jesus Christ: By whom also we have access by faith into this grace wherein we stand, and rejoice in hope of the glory of God. (Romans 5:1-2)

Rejoicing in hope; patient in tribulation; continuing instant in prayer. (Romans 12:12)

WE ARE NOT TO BE ASHAMED OF OUR HOPE

Uphold me according unto thy word, that I may live: and let me not be ashamed of my hope. (Psalm 119:116)

For I know that this shall turn to my salvation through your prayer, and the supply of the Spirit of Jesus Christ, According to my earnest expectation and my hope, that in nothing I shall be ashamed, but that with all boldness, as always, so now also Christ shall be magnified in my body, whether it be by life, or by death. (Philippians 1:19-20)

And hope maketh not ashamed; because the love of God is shed abroad in our hearts by the Holy Ghost which is given unto us. For when we were yet without strength, in due time Christ died for the ungodly. (Romans 5:5-6)

WE ARE TO LET OUR HOPE BE OUR WITNESS

But sanctify the Lord God in your hearts: and be ready always to give an answer to every man that asketh you a reason of the hope that is in you with meekness and fear. (1 Peter 3:15)

WE ARE TO USE GREAT PLAINNESS OF SPEECH AS WE HOPE

For if that which is done away was glorious, much more that which remaineth is glorious. Seeing then that we have such hope, we use great plainness of speech. (2 Corinthians 3:11-12)

WE ARE TO HOPE PATIENTLY

We give thanks to God always for you all, making mention of you in our prayers; Remembering without ceasing your work of faith, and labour of love, and patience of hope in our Lord Jesus Christ, in the sight of God and our Father. (1 Thessalonians 1:2-3)

But if we hope for that we see not, then do we with patience wait for it. (Romans 8:25)

WE ARE TO HOPE CONTINUALLY

But I will hope continually, and will yet praise thee more and more. (Psalm 71:14)

If ye continue in the faith grounded and settled, and be not moved away from the hope of the gospel, which ye have heard, and which was preached to every creature which is under heaven; whereof I Paul am made a minister. (Colossians 1:23)

WE ARE TO HAVE ONE HOPE, ONE LORD, ONE FAITH, ONE BAPTISM

Endeavouring to keep the unity of the Spirit in the bond of peace. There is one body, and one Spirit, even as ye are called in one hope of your calling; One Lord, one faith, one baptism. (Ephesians 4:3-5)

WE ARE NOT TO BE MOVED AWAY FROM OUR HOPE

If ye continue in the faith grounded and settled, and be not moved away from the hope of the gospel, which ye have heard, and which was preached to every creature which is under heaven; whereof I Paul am made a minister. (Colossians 1:23)

Hope deferred maketh the heart sick: but when the desire cometh, it is a tree of life. (Proverbs 13:12)

WE ARE TO REST IN OUR HOPE OF HIM

I have set the LORD always before me: because he is at my right hand, I shall not be moved. Therefore my heart is glad, and my glory rejoiceth: my flesh also shall rest in hope. (Psalm 16:8-9)

For David speaketh concerning him, I foresaw the Lord always before my face, for he is on my right hand, that I should not be moved: Therefore did my heart rejoice, and my tongue was glad; moreover also my flesh shall rest in hope. (Acts 2:25-26)

WE ARE TO HOPE TO THE END

And we desire that every one of you do show the same diligence to the full assurance of hope unto the end: That ye be not slothful, but followers of them who through faith and patience inherit the promises. (Hebrews 6:11-12)

But Christ as a son over his own house; whose house are we, if we hold fast the confidence and the rejoicing of the hope firm unto the end. (Hebrews 3:6)

Wherefore gird up the loins of your mind, be sober, and hope to the end for the grace that is to be brought unto you at the revelation of Jesus Christ. (1 Peter 1:13)

JESUS CHRIST—OUR BLESSED HOPE

Thus, the Bible assures believers that hope springs eternal from our Lord and Savior Jesus Christ. In Christ alone, our hope is found. He is our hope in the days and months and years to come. We hope continually because He is our eternal home. We wait quietly, patiently, and unashamedly for Him—and only Him. He is our hope—our most blessed hope.

Looking for that blessed hope, and the glorious appearing of the great God and our Saviour Jesus Christ; Who gave himself for us, that he might redeem us from all iniquity, and purify unto himself a peculiar people, zealous of good works. These things speak, and exhort, and rebuke with all authority. Let no man despise thee. (Titus 2:13-15)

CHAPTER SEVEN

REMAINING FAITHFUL THROUGH IT ALL

The hymn *Great is Thy Faithfulness* by Thomas Chisholm (1925) was inspired by Lamentations 3:22-23 and affirms that God does not change. His compassions, mercies, and love never fails. He is always faithful and true:

> Great is Thy faithfulness, O God my Father,
> There is no shadow Of turning with Thee;
> Thou changest not, Thy compassions they fail not;
> As Thou has been Thou forever shall be.

Another hymn, *It Is Well With My Soul*, written by Horatio G. Spafford (1873), affirms that whatever befalls us we remain faithful and true:

> When peace, like a river, attendeth my way,
> when sorrows like sea billows roll;
> whatever my lot, thou hast taught me to say,
> It is well, it is well with my soul.

O Come All Ye Faithful by John Francis Wade—an exhortation to the "faithful"—is underscored in this beloved Christmas carol:

> O come all ye faithful, Joyful and triumphant,
> O come ye, O come ye to Bethlehem.
> Come and behold Him, Born the King of angels.
> O come let us adore Him, O come let us adore Him,
> O come let us adore Him, Christ the Lord.

The following are selected verses about God's faithfulness to us and our need and desire to be faithful and true to Him.

GOD IS FAITHFUL TO US

GOD IS FAITHFUL

Know therefore that the LORD thy God, he is God, the faithful God, which keepeth covenant and mercy with them that love him and keep his commandments to a thousand generations. (Deuteronomy 7:9)

And I saw heaven opened, and behold a white horse; and he that sat upon him was called Faithful and True. (Revelation 19:11)

GOD'S WORD IS FAITHFUL

Holding fast the faithful word as he hath been taught, that he may be able by sound doctrine both to exhort and to convince the gainsayers. (Titus 1:9)

And he said unto me, These sayings are faithful and true: and the Lord God of the holy prophets sent his angel to show unto his servants the things which must shortly be done. Behold, I come quickly: blessed is he that keepeth the sayings of the prophecy of this book. (Revelation 22:6-7)

GOD'S FAITHFULNESS IS GREAT

It is of the LORD'S mercies that we are not consumed, because his compassions fail not. They are new every morning: great is thy faithfulness. (Lamentations 3:22-23)

GOD'S FAITHFULNESS REACHES UNTO THE CLOUDS

Thy mercy, O LORD, is in the heavens; and thy faithfulness reacheth unto the clouds.(Psalm 36:5)

GOD'S FAITHFULNESS IS UNTO ALL GENERATIONS

Thy faithfulness is unto all generations: thou hast established the earth, and it abideth. (Psalm 119:90)

GOD'S FAITHFULNESS IS IN THE CONGREGATION

And the heavens shall praise thy wonders, O LORD: thy faithfulness also in the congregation of the saints. For who in the heaven can be compared unto the LORD? who among the sons of the mighty can be likened unto the LORD? God is greatly to be feared in the assembly of the saints, and to be had in reverence of all them that are about him. O LORD God of hosts, who is a strong LORD like unto thee? or to thy faithfulness round about thee? (Psalm 89:5-8)

GOD'S FAITHFULNESS IS THE GIRDLE OF HIS REINS

And righteousness shall be the girdle of his loins, and faithfulness the girdle of his reins. (Isaiah 11:5)

GOD'S FAITHFULNESS ANSWERS PRAYERS

Hear my prayer, O LORD, give ear to my supplications: in thy faithfulness answer me, and in thy righteousness. (Psalm 143:1)

GOD'S FAITHFULNESS PROVIDES AN ESCAPE FROM TEMPTATION

There hath no temptation taken you but such as is common to man: but God is faithful, who will not suffer you to be tempted above that ye are able; but will with the temptation also make a way to escape, that ye may be able to bear it. (1 Corinthians 10:13)

GOD'S FAITHFULNESS PRESERVES THE FAITHFUL

O love the LORD, all ye his saints: for the LORD preserveth the faithful, and plentifully rewardeth the proud doer. Be of good courage, and he shall strengthen your heart, all ye that hope in the LORD. (Psalm 31:23-24)

THROUGH GOD'S FAITHFULNESS, HE FORGIVES US

If we say that we have no sin, we deceive ourselves, and the truth is not in us. If we confess our sins, he is faithful and just to forgive us our sins, and to cleanse us from all unrighteousness. (1 John 1:8-9)

GOD'S FAITHFULNESS CALLED US TO JESUS

God is faithful, by whom ye were called unto the fellowship of his Son Jesus Christ our Lord. (1 Corinthians 1:9)

Faithful is he that calleth you, who also will do it. (1 Thessalonians 5:24)

GOD'S FAITHFULNESS ESTABLISHES US

But the Lord is faithful, who shall stablish you, and keep you from evil. (2 Thessalonians 3:3)

GOD'S FAITHFULNESS ABIDES

If we believe not, yet he abideth faithful: he cannot deny himself. (2 Timothy 2:13)

GOD'S COMMANDMENTS ARE FAITHFUL

All thy commandments are faithful. (Psalm 119:86)

GOD'S TESTIMONIES ARE FAITHFUL

Righteous art thou, O LORD, and upright are thy judgments. Thy testimonies that thou hast commanded are righteous and very faithful. (Psalm 119:137-138)

GOD'S COUNSELS ARE FAITHFULNESS AND TRUTH

O LORD, thou art my God; I will exalt thee, I will praise thy name; for thou hast done wonderful things; thy counsels of old are faithfulness and truth. (Isaiah 25:1)

GOD'S SON IS THE FAITHFUL WITNESS

And from Jesus Christ, who is the faithful witness, and the first begotten of the dead, and the prince of the kings of the earth. Unto him that loved us, and washed us from our sins in his own blood, And hath made us kings and priests unto God and his Father; to him be glory and dominion for ever and ever. Amen. (Revelation 1:5-6)

JESUS' FAITHFULNESS RECONCILES US TO GOD

Wherefore in all things it behoved him to be made like unto his brethren, that he might be a merciful and faithful high priest in things pertaining to God, to make reconciliation for the sins of the people. (Hebrews 2:17)

WE ARE TO BE FAITHFUL TO GOD

WE ARE CALLED AND CHOSEN TO BE FAITHFUL

These shall make war with the Lamb, and the Lamb shall overcome them: for he is Lord of lords, and King of kings: and they that are with him are called, and chosen, and faithful. (Revelation 17:14)

OUR FAITH COMES FROM HEARING AND BELIEVING

So then faith cometh by hearing, and hearing by the word of God. (Romans 10:17)

He therefore that ministereth to you the Spirit, and worketh miracles among you, doeth he it by the works of the law, or by the hearing of faith? Even as Abraham believed God, and it was accounted to him for righteousness. Know ye therefore that they which are of faith, the same are the children of Abraham. And the scripture, foreseeing that God would justify the heathen through faith, preached before the gospel unto Abraham, saying, In thee shall all nations be blessed. So then they which be of faith are blessed with faithful Abraham. (Galatians 3:5-9)

WE ARE SAVED BY GRACE THROUGH FAITH

For by grace are ye saved through faith; and that not of yourselves: it is the gift of God: Not of works, lest any man should boast. (Ephesians 2:8-9)

OUR FAITH IS IN GOD'S SON

And that from a child thou hast known the holy scriptures, which are able to make thee wise unto salvation through faith which is in Christ Jesus. (2 Timothy 3:15)

WE ARE JUSTIFIED BY FAITH

Therefore being justified by faith, we have peace with God through our Lord Jesus Christ: By whom also we have access by faith into this grace wherein we stand, and rejoice in hope of the glory of God. (Romans 5:1-2)

Therefore we conclude that a man is justified by faith without the deeds of the law. (Romans 3:28)

THE JUST LIVE BY FAITH

Now the just shall live by faith: but if any man draw back, my soul shall have no pleasure in him. (Hebrews 10:38)

WE ARE TO HAVE FAITH IN HIS NAME

And his name through faith in his name hath made this man strong, whom ye see and know: yea, the faith which is by him hath given him this perfect soundness in the presence of you all. (Acts 3:16)

WITHOUT FAITH WE DO NOT PLEASE GOD

But without faith it is impossible to please him: for he that cometh to God must believe that he is, and that he is a rewarder of them that diligently seek him. (Hebrews 11:6)

WE ARE TO BE FAITHFUL WITH A TRUE HEART

Let us draw near with a true heart in full assurance of faith, having our hearts sprinkled from an evil conscience, and our bodies washed with pure water. (Hebrews 10:22)

WE ARE TO DECLARE GOD'S FAITHFULNESS AND LOVINGKINDNESS

I have not hid thy righteousness within my heart; I have declared thy faithfulness and thy salvation: I have not concealed thy lovingkindness and thy truth from the great congregation. (Psalm 40:10)

WE ARE TO BE FAITHFUL IN EVEN THE LEAST OF THINGS

He that is faithful in that which is least is faithful also in much: and he that is unjust in the least is unjust also in much. If therefore ye have not been faithful in the unrighteous mammon, who will commit to your trust the true riches? And if ye have not been faithful in that which is another man's, who shall give you that which is your own? (Luke 16:10-12)

His lord said unto him, Well done, good and faithful servant; thou hast been faithful over a few things, I will make thee ruler over many things: enter thou into the joy of thy lord. (Matthew 25:23)

And the Lord said, If ye had faith as a grain of mustard seed, ye might say unto this sycamine tree, Be thou plucked up by the root, and be thou planted in the sea; and it should obey you. (Luke 17:6)

OUR FAITH IS EVIDENCED BY OUR WORKS

What doth it profit, my brethren, though a man say he hath faith, and have not works? can faith save him? (James 2:14)

Even so faith, if it hath not works, is dead, being alone. (James 2:17)

For as the body without the spirit is dead, so faith without works is dead also. (James 2:26)

THE TRYING OF OUR FAITH DEVELOPS PATIENCE

My brethren, count it all joy when ye fall into divers temptations; Knowing this, that the trying of your faith worketh patience. (James 1:2-3)

THROUGH FAITH WE UNDERSTAND

Through faith we understand that the worlds were framed by the word of God, so that things which are seen were not made of things which do appear. (Hebrews 11:3)

FAITH IS THE SUBSTANCE OF THINGS HOPED FOR

Now faith is the substance of things hoped for, the evidence of things not seen. (Hebrews 11:1)

THROUGH FAITH WE INHERIT THE PROMISES

That ye be not slothful, but followers of them who through faith and patience inherit the promises. (Hebrews 6:12)

FAITHFUL FOLLOWERS ARE BLESSED

A faithful man shall abound with blessings. (Proverbs 28:20)

FAITHFUL FOLLOWERS ARE HARD TO FIND

Most men will proclaim every one his own goodness: but a faithful man who can find? (Proverbs 20:6)

WE MUST HOLD ON TO OUR FAITH

Let us hold fast the profession of our faith without wavering. (Hebrews 10:23)

Holding faith, and a good conscience; which some having put away concerning faith have made shipwreck. (1 Timothy 1:19)

WE ARE TO HAVE UNFEIGNED FAITH

Now the end of the commandment is charity out of a pure heart, and of a good conscience, and of faith unfeigned. (1 Timothy 1:5)

WE ARE TO ASK IN FAITH

If any of you lack wisdom, let him ask of God, that giveth to all men liberally, and upbraideth not; and it shall be given him. But let him ask in faith, nothing wavering. (James 1:5-6)

WE WALK BY FAITH

For we walk by faith, not by sight. (2 Corinthians 5:7)

WE ARE TO STAND FAST IN OUR FAITH

Watch ye, stand fast in the faith, quit you like men, be strong. (1 Corinthians 16:13)

Not for that we have dominion over your faith, but are helpers of your joy: for by faith ye stand. (2 Corinthians 1:24)

WE ARE TO PUT ON THE BREASTPLATE OF FAITH

But let us, who are of the day, be sober, putting on the breastplate of faith and love; and for an helmet, the hope of salvation. (1 Thessalonians 5:8)

WE ARE TO RESIST THE DEVIL WITH OUR FAITH

Be sober, be vigilant; because your adversary the devil, as a roaring lion, walketh about, seeking whom he may devour: Whom resist stedfast in the faith, knowing that the same afflictions are accomplished in your brethren that are in the world. (1 Peter 5:8-9)

Above all, taking the shield of faith, wherewith ye shall be able to quench all the fiery darts of the wicked. (Ephesians 6:16)

WE ARE TO CONTEND FOR THE FAITH

Beloved, when I gave all diligence to write unto you of the common salvation, it was needful for me to write unto you, and exhort you that ye should earnestly contend for the faith which was once delivered unto the saints. (Jude 1:3)

WE ARE TO FIGHT THE GOOD FIGHT OF FAITH

Fight the good fight of faith, lay hold on eternal life, whereunto thou art also called, and hast professed a good profession before many witnesses. (1 Timothy 6:12)

WE ARE TO FAITHFULLY WATCH FOR HIS COMING

Watch therefore: for ye know not what hour your Lord doth come. But know this, that if the goodman of the house had known in what watch the thief would come, he would have watched, and would not have suffered his house to be broken up. Therefore be ye also ready: for in such an hour as ye think not the Son of man cometh. Who then is a faithful and wise servant, whom his lord hath made ruler over his household, to give them meat in due season? Blessed is that servant, whom his lord when he cometh shall find so doing. (Matthew 24:42-46)

WE ARE TO KEEP THE FAITH

I have fought a good fight, I have finished my course, I have kept the faith. (2 Timothy 4:7)

WE ARE TO BE FAITHFUL UNTO DEATH

Fear none of those things which thou shalt suffer: behold, the devil shall cast some of you into prison, that ye may be tried; and ye shall have tribulation ten days: be thou faithful unto death, and I will give thee a crown of life. (Revelation 2:10)

FAITH OR NO FAITH?

NO FAITH

They provoked him to jealousy with strange gods, with abominations provoked they him to anger. They sacrificed unto devils, not to God; to gods whom they knew not, to new gods that came newly up, whom your fathers feared not. Of the Rock that begat thee thou art unmindful, and hast forgotten God that formed thee. And when the LORD saw it, he abhorred them, because of the provoking of his sons, and of his daughters. And he said, I will hide my face from them, I will see what their end shall be: for they are a very froward generation, children in whom is no faith. (Deuteronomy 32:16-20)

LITTLE FAITH

Wherefore, if God so clothe the grass of the field, which to day is, and to morrow is cast into the oven, shall he not much more clothe you, O ye of little faith? (Matthew 6:30)

And, behold, there arose a great tempest in the sea, insomuch that the ship was covered with the waves: but he was asleep.

And his disciples came to him, and awoke him, saying, Lord, save us: we perish. And he saith unto them, Why are ye fearful, O ye of little faith? Then he arose, and rebuked the winds and the sea; and there was a great calm. (Matthew 8:24-26)

And he said, Come. And when Peter was come down out of the ship, he walked on the water, to go to Jesus. But when he saw the wind boisterous, he was afraid; and beginning to sink, he cried, saying, Lord, save me. And immediately Jesus stretched forth his hand, and caught him, and said unto him, O thou of little faith, wherefore didst thou doubt? (Matthew 14:29-31)

FAITHFUL THAT FAIL

Help, LORD; for the godly man ceaseth; for the faithful fail from among the children of men. They speak vanity every one with his neighbour: with flattering lips and with a double heart do they speak. (Psalm 12:1-2)

DEPARTING FROM THE FAITH

Now the Spirit speaketh expressly, that in the latter times some shall depart from the faith, giving heed to seducing spirits, and doctrines of devils. (1 Timothy 4:1)

FAITH WHEN HE RETURNS?

In Luke 18:7-8, there is a strong intimation that when Jesus returns there may not be much faith on the earth.

And shall not God avenge his own elect, which cry day and night unto him, though he bear long with them? I tell you that he will avenge them speedily. Nevertheless when the Son of man cometh, shall he find faith on the earth?

When the disciples ask Jesus what will be the sign of His return, the very first sign he discloses is deception—that people will be deceived away from the true faith by of those who will come in His name claiming to be Christians and claiming to be Christ:

> And as he sat upon the mount of Olives, the disciples came unto him privately, saying, Tell us, when shall these things be? and what shall be the sign of thy coming, and of the end of the world? And Jesus answered and said unto them, Take heed that no man deceive you. For many shall come in my name, saying, I am Christ; and shall deceive many. (Matthew 24:3-5)

> And many false prophets shall rise, and shall deceive many. (Matthew 24:11)

> For there shall arise false Christs, and false prophets, and shall show great signs and wonders; insomuch that, if it were possible, they shall deceive the very elect. Behold, I have told you before. Wherefore if they shall say unto you, Behold, he is in the desert; go not forth: behold, he is in the secret chambers; believe it not. (Matthew 24:24-26)

God warns in Scripture of a great Last Days deception, but exhorts us to press on, contending for the faith, fighting the good fight of faith, keeping the faith, and remaining faithful to the very end. He assures us that His grace is sufficient and that—through it all—He will help us and preserve us if we but wait and entrust ourselves to Him in faith:

> And he said unto me, My grace is sufficient for thee: for my strength is made perfect in weakness. (2 Corinthians 12:9)

> O love the LORD, all ye his saints: for the LORD preserveth the faithful, and plentifully rewardeth the proud doer. Be of good courage, and he shall strengthen your heart, all ye that hope in the LORD. (Psalm 31:23-24)

> Hast thou not known? hast thou not heard, that the everlasting God, the LORD, the Creator of the ends of the earth, fainteth not, neither is weary? there is no searching of his understanding.

He giveth power to the faint; and to them that have no might he increaseth strength. Even the youths shall faint and be weary, and the young men shall utterly fall: But they that wait upon the LORD shall renew their strength; they shall mount up with wings as eagles; they shall run, and not be weary; and they shall walk, and not faint. (Isaiah 40:28-31)

TO THOSE WHO REMAIN FAITHFUL

Amazingly, to God's praise and glory, we can be confidant that He will be faithful to complete the work that He has begun in us:

Being confident of this very thing, that he which hath begun a good work in you will perform it until the day of Jesus Christ. (Philippians 1:6)

Also amazingly and to His praise and glory, is what awaits those who love Him, wait for Him, and remain faithful to Him:

But as it is written, Eye hath not seen, nor ear heard, neither have entered into the heart of man, the things which God hath prepared for them that love him. (1 Corinthians 2:9)

And perhaps most amazing of all are the words the faithful will one day hear from Him Who has always been faithful and true to us:

Well done, thou good and faithful servant. (Matthew 25:21)

CHAPTER EIGHT

REJOICING THROUGH IT ALL

A s challenging as it may seem at times, God's Word tells us to rejoice always (Philippians 4:4) and evermore (1 Thessalonians 5:16). The various Hebrew and Greek words for rejoicing range in meaning from calmly happy to exceedingly glad and jumping for joy. The Bible reminds us that God's people should be a "happy" people because our God is the Lord (Psalm 144:15). We know that "though our outward man perish" yet our "inward man is renewed day by day." Therefore, we rejoice and give thanks for the "abundant grace" so mercifully bestowed upon us by God our Savior.

> Knowing that he which raised up the Lord Jesus shall raise up us also by Jesus, and shall present us with you. For all things are for your sakes, that the abundant grace might through the thanksgiving of many redound to the glory of God. For which cause we faint not; but though our outward man perish, yet the inward man is renewed day by day. (2 Corinthians 4:14-16)

WHY DO WE REJOICE?

The old revered hymn *Count Your Blessings* by Johnson Oatman (1897) reminds us that even in our darkest moments we are to rejoice and count our many blessings:

> When upon life's billows you are tempest tossed,
> When you are discouraged, thinking all is lost,
> Count your many blessings, name them one by one,
> And it will surprise you what the Lord hath done.

There are so many blessings and so many reasons why we should rejoice always and evermore. Here are just a few:

JESUS CHRIST CAME INTO THE WORLD TO BE OUR SAVIOR

And the angel said unto them, Fear not: for, behold, I bring you good tidings of great joy, which shall be to all people. For unto you is born this day in the city of David a Saviour, which is Christ the Lord. (Luke 2:10-11)

HIS NAME IS ABOVE ALL NAMES

Wherefore God also hath highly exalted him, and given him a name which is above every name: That at the name of Jesus every knee should bow, of things in heaven, and things in earth, and things under the earth; And that every tongue should confess that Jesus Christ is Lord, to the glory of God the Father. (Philippians 2:9-11)

ALL THINGS WERE CREATED BY HIM

In the beginning was the Word, and the Word was with God, and the Word was God. The same was in the beginning with God. All things were made by him; and without him was not any thing made that was made. (John 1:1-3)

For by him were all things created, that are in heaven, and that are in earth, visible and invisible, whether they be thrones, or dominions, or principalities, or powers: all things were created by him, and for him: And he is before all things, and by him all things consist. (Colossians 1:16-17)

JESUS IS THE PROPITIATION FOR OUR SINS

And he is the propitiation for our sins: and not for ours only, but also for the sins of the whole world. (1 John 2:2)

But God commendeth his love toward us, in that, while we were yet sinners, Christ died for us. (Romans 5:8)

Giving thanks unto the Father, which hath made us meet to be partakers of the inheritance of the saints in light: Who hath delivered us from the power of darkness, and hath translated us into the kingdom of his dear Son: In whom we have redemption through his blood, even the forgiveness of sins. (Colossians 1:12-14)

HE DEFEATED SIN AND SATAN AND DEATH ON THE CROSS OF CALVARY

Forasmuch then as the children are partakers of flesh and blood, he also himself likewise took part of the same; that through death he might destroy him that had the power of death, that is, the devil. (Hebrews 2:14)

HE HAS GIVEN US THE VICTORY

But thanks be to God, which giveth us the victory through our Lord Jesus Christ. (1 Corinthians 15:57)

WE ARE SAVED BECAUSE OF HIM

That if thou shalt confess with thy mouth the Lord Jesus, and shalt believe in thine heart that God hath raised him from the dead, thou shalt be saved. (Romans 10:9)

WE HAVE BEEN SAVED BY HIS GRACE ALONE

For by grace are ye saved through faith; and that not of yourselves: it is the gift of God: Not of works, lest any man should boast. (Ephesians 2:8-9)

WE ARE THE CHILDREN OF GOD THROUGH FAITH IN HIM

For ye are all the children of God by faith in Christ Jesus. (Galatians 3:26)

WE HAVE PEACE WITH GOD THROUGH HIM

Therefore being justified by faith, we have peace with God through our Lord Jesus Christ. (Romans 5:1)

HE GAVE US HIS LIFE

Hereby perceive we the love of God, because he laid down his life for us: and we ought to lay down our lives for the brethren. (1 John 3:16)

HE GAVE US HIS WORD

All scripture is given by inspiration of God, and is profitable for doctrine, for reproof, for correction, for instruction in righteousness: That the man of God may be perfect, thoroughly furnished unto all good works. (2 Timothy 3:16-17)

HE HAS GIVEN US THE GIFT OF EVERLASTING LIFE

For God so loved the world, that he gave his only begotten Son, that whosoever believeth in him should not perish, but have everlasting life. (John 3:16)

HOW DO WE REJOICE?

WE REJOICE FOR THIS DAY

This is the day which the LORD hath made; we will rejoice and be glad in it. (Psalm 118:24)

WE REJOICE IN GOD'S SALVATION

We will rejoice in thy salvation, and in the name of our God we will set up our banners. (Psalm 20:5)

And it shall be said in that day, Lo, this is our God; we have waited for him, and he will save us: this is the LORD; we have waited for him, we will be glad and rejoice in his salvation. (Isaiah 25:9)

Lest mine enemy say, I have prevailed against him; and those that trouble me rejoice when I am moved. But I have trusted in thy mercy; my heart shall rejoice in thy salvation. I will sing unto the LORD, because he hath dealt bountifully with me. (Psalm 13:4-6)

The voice of rejoicing and salvation is in the tabernacles of the righteous. (Psalm 118:15)

WE REJOICE THAT GOD HAS CLOTHED US WITH THE GARMENTS OF SALVATION

I will greatly rejoice in the LORD, my soul shall be joyful in my God; for he hath clothed me with the garments of salvation, he hath covered me with the robe of righteousness, as a bridegroom decketh himself with ornaments, and as a bride adorneth herself with her jewels. (Isaiah 61:10)

WE REJOICE IN CHRIST JESUS

For we are the circumcision, which worship God in the spirit, and rejoice in Christ Jesus, and have no confidence in the flesh. (Philippians 3:3)

WE REJOICE IN HIS NAME

For our heart shall rejoice in him, because we have trusted in his holy name. (Psalm 33:21)

In thy name shall they rejoice all the day: and in thy righteousness shall they be exalted. (Psalm 89:16)

WE REJOICE AND SING PRAISE TO HIS NAME

I will be glad and rejoice in thee: I will sing praise to thy name, O thou most High. (Psalm 9:2)

Sing unto God, sing praises to his name: extol him that rideth upon the heavens by his name JAH, and rejoice before him. (Psalm 68:4)

WE REJOICE AS WE SEEK THE LORD

Let all those that seek thee rejoice and be glad in thee: let such as love thy salvation say continually, The LORD be magnified. (Psalm 40:16)

WE REJOICE IN SUFFERING FOR HIS NAME

And they departed from the presence of the council, rejoicing that they were counted worthy to suffer shame for his name. (Acts 5:41)

WE REJOICE IN GOD'S WORD

I rejoice at thy word, as one that findeth great spoil. (Psalm 119:162)

WE REJOICE IN HIS TESTIMONIES

I have rejoiced in the way of thy testimonies, as much as in all riches. (Psalm 119:14)

WE REJOICE IN HIS STATUTES

The statutes of the LORD are right, rejoicing the heart: the commandment of the LORD is pure, enlightening the eyes. (Psalm 19:8)

WE REJOICE IN THE TRUTH

Rejoiceth not in iniquity, but rejoiceth in the truth. (1 Corinthians 13:6)

WE REJOICE WHEN OTHERS WALK IN TRUTH

I rejoiced greatly that I found of thy children walking in truth as we have received a commandment from the Father. (2 John 1:4)

WE REJOICE EVEN IN HEAVINESS

Wherein ye greatly rejoice, though now for a season, if need be, ye are in heaviness through manifold temptations. (1 Peter 1:6)

WE REJOICE EVEN IN SORROW

As sorrowful, yet alway rejoicing; as poor, yet making many rich; as having nothing, and yet possessing all things. (2 Corinthians 6:10)

WE REJOICE WHEN WE PARTAKE IN CHRIST'S SUFFERINGS

Beloved, think it not strange concerning the fiery trial which is to try you, as though some strange thing happened unto you: But rejoice, inasmuch as ye are partakers of Christ's sufferings; that, when his glory shall be revealed, ye may be glad also with exceeding joy. If ye be reproached for the name of Christ, happy are ye; for the spirit of glory and of God resteth upon you: on their part he is evil spoken of, but on your part he is glorified. (1 Peter 4:12-14)

WE REJOICE EVEN THOUGH WE DON'T SEE HIM

That the trial of your faith, being much more precious than of gold that perisheth, though it be tried with fire, might be found unto praise and honour and glory at the appearing of Jesus Christ: Whom having not seen, ye love; in whom, though now ye see him not, yet believing, ye rejoice with joy unspeakable and full of glory. (1 Peter 1:7-8)

WE REJOICE IN GOD'S MERCY

I will be glad and rejoice in thy mercy: for thou hast considered my trouble; thou hast known my soul in adversities. (Psalm 31:7)

WE REJOICE WITH TREMBLING

Serve the LORD with fear, and rejoice with trembling. (Psalm 2:11)

WE REJOICE BECAUSE GOD IS OUR HELP

Because thou hast been my help, therefore in the shadow of thy wings will I rejoice. (Psalm 63:7)

WE REJOICE BUT REMAIN ALERT FOR EVIL WORKERS

Finally, my brethren, rejoice in the Lord. To write the same things to you, to me indeed is not grievous, but for you it is safe. Beware of dogs, beware of evil workers. (Philippians 3:1-2)

WE REJOICE BECAUSE WE TRUST IN THE LORD AND HE DEFENDS US

But let all those that put their trust in thee rejoice: let them ever shout for joy, because thou defendest them. (Psalm 5:11)

The LORD is my strength and my shield; my heart trusted in him, and I am helped: therefore my heart greatly rejoiceth; and with my song will I praise him. (Psalm 28:7)

WE REJOICE IN THE LORD ALWAYS

Rejoice in the Lord alway: and again I say, Rejoice. (Philippians 4:4)

WE REJOICE BUT WE DO NOT FORGET THE DAYS OF DARKNESS

But if a man live many years, and rejoice in them all; yet let him remember the days of darkness; for they shall be many. All that cometh is vanity. (Ecclesiastes 11:8)

WE REJOICE WHEN WE ARE HATED AND REPROACHED

Blessed are ye, when men shall hate you, and when they shall separate you from their company, and shall reproach you, and cast out your name as evil, for the Son of man's sake. Rejoice ye in that day, and leap for joy: for, behold, your reward is great in heaven: for in the like manner did their fathers unto the prophets. (Luke 6:22-23)

WE REJOICE WHEN WE ARE PERSECUTED

Blessed are they which are persecuted for righteousness' sake: for theirs is the kingdom of heaven. Blessed are ye, when men shall revile you, and persecute you, and shall say all manner of evil against you falsely, for my sake. Rejoice, and be exceeding glad: for great is your reward in heaven: for so persecuted they the prophets which were before you. (Matthew 5:10-12)

WE REJOICE WHEN THERE SEEMS LITTLE TO REJOICE ABOUT

Although the fig tree shall not blossom, neither shall fruit be in the vines; the labour of the olive shall fail, and the fields shall yield no meat; the flock shall be cut off from the fold, and there shall be no herd in the stalls: Yet I will rejoice in the LORD, I will joy in the God of my salvation. The LORD God is my strength, and he will make my feet like hinds' feet, and he will make me to walk upon mine high places. (Habakkuk 3:17-19)

WE REJOICE BEFORE GOD

But let the righteous be glad; let them rejoice before God: yea, let them exceedingly rejoice. (Psalm 68:3)

WE REJOICE WHEN THE RIGHTEOUS ARE IN AUTHORITY

When the righteous are in authority, the people rejoice: but when the wicked beareth rule, the people mourn. (Proverbs 29:2)

WE REJOICE AND MAKE A JOYFUL NOISE

Make a joyful noise unto the LORD, all the earth: make a loud noise, and rejoice, and sing praise. (Psalm 98:4)

WE REJOICE IN HOPE

[W]e have peace with God through our Lord Jesus Christ: By whom also we have access by faith into this grace wherein we stand, and rejoice in hope of the glory of God. (Romans 5:1-2)

WE REJOICE WHEN WE ARE REVIVED

Wilt thou not revive us again: that thy people may rejoice in thee? (Psalm 85:6)

WE REJOICE IN THE LORD AND SHOUT FOR JOY

Be glad in the LORD, and rejoice, ye righteous: and shout for joy, all ye that are upright in heart. (Psalm 32:11)

WE REJOICE WITH THEM THAT REJOICE AND WEEP WITH THEM THAT WEEP

Rejoice with them that do rejoice, and weep with them that weep. (Romans 12:15)

WE REJOICE AFTER SOWING IN TEARS

He that goeth forth and weepeth, bearing precious seed, shall doubtless come again with rejoicing, bringing his sheaves with him. (Psalm 126:6)

WE REJOICE BECAUSE JESUS WENT TO THE FATHER

Peace I leave with you, my peace I give unto you: not as the world giveth, give I unto you. Let not your heart be troubled, neither let it be afraid. Ye have heard how I said unto you, I go away, and come again unto you. If ye loved me, ye would rejoice, because I said, I go unto the Father: for my Father is greater than I. (John 14:27-28)

WE REJOICE AND WE SUFFER WITH THE BODY OF CHRIST

And whether one member suffer, all the members suffer with it; or one member be honoured, all the members rejoice with it. (1 Corinthians 12:26)

WE REJOICE WHEN CHRIST IS PREACHED

What then? notwithstanding, every way, whether in pretence, or in truth, Christ is preached; and I therein do rejoice, yea, and will rejoice. (Philippians 1:18)

WE REJOICE IN EVERY GOOD THING THE LORD GIVES US

And thou shalt rejoice in every good thing which the LORD thy God hath given unto thee. (Deuteronomy 26:11)

WE REJOICE AND GIVE THANKS FOR HIS HOLINESS

Rejoice in the LORD, ye righteous; and give thanks at the remembrance of his holiness. (Psalm 97:12)

WE DECLARE HIS WORKS WITH REJOICING

Oh that men would praise the LORD for his goodness, and for his wonderful works to the children of men! And let them sacrifice the sacrifices of thanksgiving, and declare his works with rejoicing. (Psalm 107:21-22)

WE REJOICE THAT OUR NAMES ARE WRITTEN IN HEAVEN

Notwithstanding in this rejoice not, that the spirits are subject unto you; but rather rejoice, because your names are written in heaven. (Luke 10:20)

WE REJOICE IN THE DAY OF CHRIST

Do all things without murmurings and disputings: That ye may be blameless and harmless, the sons of God, without rebuke, in the midst of a crooked and perverse nation, among whom ye shine as lights in the world; Holding forth the word of life;

that I may rejoice in the day of Christ, that I have not run in vain, neither laboured in vain. (Philippians 2:14-16)

WE REJOICE IN THE NEW HEAVENS, THE NEW EARTH, AND THE NEW JERUSALEM

For, behold, I create new heavens and a new earth: and the former shall not be remembered, nor come into mind. But be ye glad and rejoice for ever in that which I create: for, behold, I create Jerusalem a rejoicing, and her people a joy. And I will rejoice in Jerusalem, and joy in my people: and the voice of weeping shall be no more heard in her, nor the voice of crying. (Isaiah 65:17-19)

WE REJOICE RIGHT TO THE END

But Christ as a son over his own house; whose house are we, if we hold fast the confidence and the rejoicing of the hope firm unto the end. (Hebrews 3:6)

WE REJOICE EVERMORE

Rejoice evermore. (1 Thessalonians 5:16)

BEWARE OF FALSE REJOICING

While Scripture tells us to rejoice in the Lord always and evermore, we are *not* to rejoice in things that are not from God. In today's church, false teachers, false teachings, and false Christs abound. Godly rejoicing is based on a true relationship with our true Lord and Savior Jesus Christ. True rejoicing is the inward and outward expression of the Holy Spirit within us. We rejoice that the joy of the Lord is our strength (Nehemiah 8:10). Godly rejoicing takes place in all circumstances—no matter what. It says in spite of everything, the Lord is with us and "it is well with my soul." However, the city of Nineveh is a classic example of ungodly false rejoicing:

This is the rejoicing city that dwelt carelessly, that said in her heart, I am, and there is none beside me: how is she become a desolation, a place for beasts to lie down in every one that passeth by her shall hiss, and wag his hand. (Zephaniah 2:15)

The Bible warns us that we can be "zealously" affected by things that are *not* of God (Galatians 4:17). As with Nineveh, Israel's ungodly false rejoicing also led to severe consequences:

Therefore my people are gone into captivity, because they have no knowledge: and their honourable men are famished, and their multitude dried up with thirst. Therefore hell hath enlarged herself, and opened her mouth without measure: and their glory, and their multitude, and their pomp, and he that rejoiceth, shall descend into it. (Isaiah 5:13-14)

In Revelation 3:1, Jesus underscored how the church in Sardis had a reputation for being spiritually "alive," when in reality, it was spiritually "dead."

And unto the angel of the church in Sardis write; These things saith he that hath the seven Spirits of God, and the seven stars; I know thy works, that thou hast a name that thou livest, and art dead. (Revelation 3:1)

Let us not be deceived. Jesus warned that worldwide deception—not worldwide rejoicing and worldwide revival—would be *the* chief sign at the end of time (Matthew 24:3-5). While New Age teachers proclaim the coming of a great "Global Spiritual Awakening" and a "Planetary Pentecost," deceived Christian leaders similarly proclaim the coming of a great "Global Spiritual Awakening" and a "Second Pentecost." However, the Bible warns of global deception, the coming of Antichrist, and a planetary holocaust.

There is no legitimate worldwide revival poised on the threshold ready to break forth. What we are told in Scripture—if we choose to believe it—is that "evil men and seducers shall wax worse and worse." Yet, in spite of it all—and through it all—we are to rejoice in our Lord God who has mercifully warned us that these events will definitely transpire. His warnings are not intended to frighten or intimidate us, but to prepare us for what lies ahead. We are to continue in our faith and in the things of which we have learned and been assured. The apostle Paul states:

> Yea, and all that will live godly in Christ Jesus shall suffer persecution. But evil men and seducers shall wax worse and worse, deceiving, and being deceived. But continue thou in the things which thou hast learned and hast been assured of, knowing of whom thou hast learned them. (2 Timothy 3:10-14)

TRUE REJOICING

People involved in true rejoicing expose false teachers rather than joining forces with them. They reprove spiritual deception rather than becoming a part of it. People involved in true rejoicing fear God, keep His Word, and do not look for signs and wonders or get involved in false rejoicing or false revival. They "rejoiceth not in iniquity but rejoiceth in the truth." They celebrate the truth, the whole truth, and nothing but the truth. People involved in true rejoicing endeavor to rejoice always and evermore.

> Let the heavens be glad, and let the earth rejoice: and let men say among the nations, The LORD reigneth. Let the sea roar, and the fulness thereof: let the fields rejoice, and all that is therein. Then shall the trees of the wood sing out at the presence of the LORD, because he cometh to judge the earth. O give thanks unto the LORD; for he is good; for his mercy endureth for ever. (1 Chronicles 16:31-34)

CHAPTER NINE

SOUND DOCTRINE THROUGH IT ALL

Give ear, O ye heavens, and I will speak; and hear, O earth, the words of my mouth. My doctrine shall drop as the rain, my speech shall distil as the dew, as the small rain upon the tender herb, and as the showers upon the grass. (Deuteronomy 32:1-2)

How precious is the Book divine, by inspiration given! Bright as a lamp its doctrines shine, to guide our souls to heaven.

—John Fawcett
How Precious is the Book Divine (1782)

DOCTRINE AND DOGMA

t is not very popular these days, but the Bible tells us to *study* and to *rightly divide* the Word of God:

Study to shew thyself approved unto God, a workman that needeth not to be ashamed, rightly dividing the word of truth. (2 Timothy 2:15)

Scripture tells us that the Word of God is "quick, and powerful, and sharper than any two-edged sword":

> For the word of God is quick, and powerful, and sharper than any twoedged sword, piercing even to the dividing asunder of soul and spirit, and of the joints and marrow, and is a discerner of the thoughts and intents of the heart. (Hebrews 4:12)

Scripture assures us that God's Word *really* is God's inspired Word, and that it is profitable for doctrine:

> All scripture is given by inspiration of God, and is profitable for doctrine, for reproof, for correction, for instruction in righteousness: That the man of God may be perfect, thoroughly furnished unto all good works. (2 Timothy 3:16-17)

But in the deceptive times in which we live, doctrine has become, for many, a harsh and even hated word. Yet, according to *Strong's Concordance,* the word doctrine in Greek simply refers to "instruction" and "teaching." *Webster's New American Dictionary* defines doctrine as "something taught as the principles or creed of a religion, political party, etc.; tenet or tenets; belief; dogma." The word dogma also takes a bad rap and is similarly defined by Webster as "a belief or set of beliefs that is accepted by the members of a group without being questioned or doubted." These definitions are very straightforward, but the words doctrine and dogma still carry heavy negative connotations—even in the minds of many believers. If someone holds to doctrinal truth and refuses to compromise, they are frequently regarded as being too "dogmatic" and "hung up on doctrine."

SPIRITUAL EXPERIENCES

Today, spiritual experience is taking precedent over sound doctrine, and it is leading to great deception in the church. Having an "encounter" with God has become more of a priority than knowing and rightly dividing the Word of God. And in the process, deceptive spirits have moved into the lives of undiscerning believers as they temptingly offer counterfeit spiritual experiences—all in the name of "God," "Jesus," and the "Holy Spirit." And this is exactly what the Bible said would happen in these last days:

> Now the Spirit speaketh expressly, that in the latter times some shall depart from the faith, giving heed to seducing spirits, and doctrines of devils. (1 Timothy 4:1)

> For the time will come when they will not endure sound doctrine; but after their own lusts shall they heap to themselves teachers, having itching ears; And they shall turn away their ears from the truth, and shall be turned unto fables. (2 Timothy 4:3-4)

The word doctrine is specifically cited in the New Testament forty-nine times. Any teaching—especially whatever comes through personal experience as seemingly "new revelation," "new truth," or "new doctrine," must always be measured by God's Holy Word (Acts 17:11) and spiritually tested for truth and authenticity (1 John 4:1-3). Not every spiritual encounter is from God. There is a deceiver. The following selected Bible verses underline the importance of sound doctrine and the necessity of keeping, abiding, and holding fast to God's Word.

BIBLE DOCTRINE

ALL SCRIPTURE IS PROFITABLE FOR DOCTRINE

All scripture is given by inspiration of God, and is profitable for doctrine, for reproof, for correction, for instruction in righteousness: That the man of God may be perfect, thoroughly furnished unto all good works. (2 Timothy 3:16-17)

JESUS TAUGHT DOCTRINE

And he began again to teach by the sea side: and there was gathered unto him a great multitude, so that he entered into a ship, and sat in the sea; and the whole multitude was by the sea on the land. And he taught them many things by parables, and said unto them in his doctrine. (Mark 4:1-2)

And he said unto them in his doctrine, Beware of the scribes, which love to go in long clothing, and love salutations in the marketplaces. (Mark 12:38)

The high priest then asked Jesus of his disciples, and of his doctrine. Jesus answered him, I spake openly to the world; I ever taught in the synagogue, and in the temple, whither the Jews always resort; and in secret have I said nothing. Why askest thou me? ask them which heard me, what I have said unto them: behold, they know what I said. (John 18:19-21)

PEOPLE WERE ASTONISHED AT JESUS' DOCTRINE

And it came to pass, when Jesus had ended these sayings, the people were astonished at his doctrine: For he taught them as one having authority, and not as the scribes. (Matthew 7:28-29)

And the scribes and chief priests heard it, and sought how they might destroy him: for they feared him, because all the people was astonished at his doctrine. (Mark 11:18)

And came down to Capernaum, a city of Galilee, and taught them on the sabbath days. And they were astonished at his doctrine: for his word was with power. (Luke 4:31-32)

JESUS' DOCTRINE WAS GOD'S DOCTRINE

Now about the midst of the feast Jesus went up into the temple, and taught. And the Jews marvelled, saying, How knoweth this man letters, having never learned? Jesus answered them, and said, My doctrine is not mine, but his that sent me. (John 7:14-16)

GOD'S DOCTRINE WAS DELIVERED TO THE CHURCH

But God be thanked, that ye were the servants of sin, but ye have obeyed from the heart that form of doctrine which was delivered you. (Romans 6:17)

GOD'S DOCTRINE IS GOOD DOCTRINE

Hear, ye children, the instruction of a father, and attend to know understanding. For I give you good doctrine, forsake ye not my law. (Proverbs 4:1-2)

GOD'S DOCTRINE IS TO BE UNDERSTOOD AND LEARNED

They also that erred in spirit shall come to understanding, and they that murmured shall learn doctrine. (Isaiah 29:24)

Whom shall he teach knowledge? and whom shall he make to understand doctrine? them that are weaned from the milk, and drawn from the breasts. For precept must be upon precept, precept upon precept; line upon line, line upon line; here a little, and there a little. (Isaiah 28:9-10)

GOD'S DOCTRINE NOURISHES

If thou put the brethren in remembrance of these things, thou shalt be a good minister of Jesus Christ, nourished up in the words of faith and of good doctrine, whereunto thou hast attained. (1 Timothy 4:6)

GOD'S DOCTRINE EDIFIES

How is it then, brethren? when ye come together, every one of you hath a psalm, hath a doctrine, hath a tongue, hath a revelation, hath an interpretation. Let all things be done unto edifying. (1 Corinthians 14:26)

LABORING IN DOCTRINE IS HONORABLE

Let the elders that rule well be counted worthy of double honour, especially they who labour in the word and doctrine.

For the scripture saith, Thou shalt not muzzle the ox that treadeth out the corn. And, The labourer is worthy of his reward. (1 Timothy 5:17-18)

GOOD WORKS COME FROM GOOD DOCTRINE

In all things showing thyself a pattern of good works: in doctrine showing uncorruptness, gravity, sincerity. (Titus 2:7)

WE ARE TO ATTEND TO DOCTRINE

Till I come, give attendance to reading, to exhortation, to doctrine. (1 Timothy 4:13)

WE ARE TO SPEAK SOUND DOCTRINE

But speak thou the things which become sound doctrine. (Titus 2:1)

WE ARE TO EXHORT WITH SOUND DOCTRINE

Holding fast the faithful word as he hath been taught, that he may be able by sound doctrine both to exhort and to convince the gainsayers. (Titus 1:9)

Preach the word; be instant in season, out of season; reprove, rebuke, exhort with all longsuffering and doctrine. (2 Timothy 4:3)

WE ARE TO ADORN DOCTRINE IN ALL THINGS

Not purloining, but showing all good fidelity; that they may adorn the doctrine of God our Saviour in all things. (Titus 2:10)

WE ARE TO TEACH NO OTHER DOCTRINE

As I besought thee to abide still at Ephesus, when I went into Macedonia, that thou mightest charge some that they teach no other doctrine. (1 Timothy 1:3)

WE ARE TO BEWARE OF THE DOCTRINES OF MEN

Then Jesus said unto them, Take heed and beware of the leaven of the Pharisees and of the Sadducees. . . . How is it that ye do not understand that I spake it not to you concerning bread, that ye should beware of the leaven of the Pharisees and of the Sadducees? Then understood they how that he bade them not beware of the leaven of bread, but of the doctrine of the Pharisees and of the Sadducees. (Matthew 16:6, 11-12)

Wherefore if ye be dead with Christ from the rudiments of the world, why, as though living in the world, are ye subject to ordinances, (Touch not; taste not; handle not; Which all are to perish with the using;) after the commandments and doctrines of men? Which things have indeed a shew of wisdom in will worship, and humility, and neglecting of the body; not in any honour to the satisfying of the flesh. (Colossians 2:20-23)

WE ARE NOT TO TEACH THE DOCTRINES OF MEN

Ye hypocrites, well did Esaias prophesy of you, saying, This people draweth nigh unto me with their mouth, and honoureth me with their lips; but their heart is far from me. But in vain they do worship me, teaching for doctrines the commandments of men. (Matthew 15:7-9)

WE MUST BEWARE OF FALSE DOCTRINE

Now I beseech you, brethren, mark them which cause divisions and offences contrary to the doctrine which ye have learned; and avoid them. For they that are such serve not our Lord Jesus Christ, but their own belly; and by good words and fair speeches deceive the hearts of the simple. (Romans 16:17-18)

Knowing this, that the law is not made for a righteous man, but for the lawless and disobedient, for the ungodly and for sinners, for unholy and profane, for murderers of fathers and murderers of mothers, for manslayers, For whoremongers, for them that defile themselves with mankind, for menstealers, for liars, for perjured persons, and if there be any other thing that is contrary to sound doctrine; According to the glorious gospel of the blessed God, which was committed to my trust. (1 Timothy 1:9-11)

WE ARE TO CONTINUE IN DOCTRINE

Then they that gladly received his word were baptized: and the same day there were added unto them about three thousand souls. And they continued stedfastly in the apostles' doctrine and fellowship, and in breaking of bread, and in prayers. (Acts 2:41-42)

Take heed unto thyself, and unto the doctrine; continue in them: for in doing this thou shalt both save thyself, and them that hear thee. (1 Timothy 4:16)

WE ARE NOT TO BE CARRIED AWAY WITH FALSE DOCTRINES

Jesus Christ the same yesterday, and to day, and for ever. Be not carried about with divers and strange doctrines. (Hebrews 13:8-9)

That we henceforth be no more children, tossed to and fro, and carried about with every wind of doctrine, by the sleight of men, and cunning craftiness, whereby they lie in wait to deceive. (Ephesians 4:14)

WE MUST REMOVE OURSELVES FROM THOSE WHO TEACH FALSE DOCTRINES

If any man teach otherwise, and consent not to wholesome words, even the words of our Lord Jesus Christ, and to the doctrine which is according to godliness; He is proud, knowing nothing, but doting about questions and strifes of words, whereof cometh envy, strife, railings, evil surmisings, Perverse disputings of men of corrupt minds, and destitute of the truth, supposing that gain is godliness: from such withdraw thyself. But godliness with contentment is great gain. (1 Timothy 6:3-6)

SOUND DOCTRINE WILL NOT BE ENDURED

For the time will come when they will not endure sound doctrine; but after their own lusts shall they heap to themselves teachers, having itching ears; And they shall turn away their ears from the truth, and shall be turned unto fables. (2 Timothy 4:3-4)

WE MUST NOT GIVE HEED TO SEDUCING SPIRITS AND DOCTRINES OF DEVILS

Now the Spirit speaketh expressly, that in the latter times some shall depart from the faith, giving heed to seducing spirits, and doctrines of devils. (1 Timothy 4:1)

WE MUST ABIDE IN THE DOCTRINE OF CHRIST

Whosoever transgresseth, and abideth not in the doctrine of Christ, hath not God. He that abideth in the doctrine of Christ, he hath both the Father and the Son. If there come any unto you, and bring not this doctrine, receive him not into your house, neither bid him God speed: For he that biddeth him God speed is partaker of his evil deeds. (2 John 1:9-11)

WE MUST BEWARE OF DOCTRINES OF VANITIES

But they are altogether brutish and foolish: the stock is a doctrine of vanities. (Jeremiah 10:8)

WE MUST REPENT OF FALSE DOCTRINES

But I have a few things against thee, because thou hast there them that hold the doctrine of Balaam, who taught Balac to cast a stumblingblock before the children of Israel, to eat things sacrificed unto idols, and to commit fornication. So hast thou also them that hold the doctrine of the Nicolaitanes, which thing I hate. Repent; or else I will come unto thee quickly, and will fight against them with the sword of my mouth. (Revelation 2:14-16)

CONCLUSION

In a period of time when the Word of God is being discounted, denigrated, and deconstructed, it is especially important that we hold fast to the Word of God and the doctrines it espouses. The Bible states that "blessed are they that hear the word of God, and keep it" (Luke 11:28). The Bereans were commended by the apostle Paul because "they received the word with all readiness of mind, and searched the scriptures daily" to see whether the things they were being taught and told "were so" (Acts 17:11). May God bless and keep you as you search the Scriptures and endeavor to stand fast on the Bible's inspired teachings and inspired sound doctrines.

A PRAYER

I have rejoiced in the way of thy testimonies, as much as in all riches. I will meditate in thy precepts, and have respect unto thy ways. I will delight myself in thy statutes: I will not forget thy word. Deal bountifully with thy servant, that I may live, and keep thy word. (Psalm 119:14-17)

CHAPTER TEN

STANDING FAST
THROUGH IT ALL

If thou faint in the day of adversity, thy strength is small. (Proverbs 24:10)

Hostility towards those who hold fast to the Lord Jesus Christ and the literal teachings of the Bible has increased greatly. Biblical Christians endeavoring to stand in their faith have been shocked and saddened at the growing antagonism coming at them not only from the world but from within the professing church itself. This booklet will attempt to convey what Scripture tells us about remaining faithful in the midst of this spiritual opposition—what to expect and how to respond.

STANDING

Standing is to be stationary; to persevere, to endure, to stand fast. While the world moves "forward" with its distorted agenda, God's people are exhorted to *stand fast* in their faith as they *stand against* false teachings and the wiles of the Devil.

Therefore, brethren, stand fast, and hold the traditions which ye have been taught, whether by word, or our epistle. (2 Thessalonians 2:15)

Finally, my brethren, be strong in the Lord, and in the power of his might. Put on the whole armour of God, that ye may be able to stand against the wiles of the devil. (Ephesians 6:10-11)

STEADFAST

The act of standing fast is to be steadfast. Steadfast means firm, fixed, settled, or established. Not changing, fickle or wavering; constant. As believers, we are to remain steadfast and unmoveable in our faith as we resist the Devil and the temptations of the world.

Therefore, my beloved brethren, be ye stedfast, unmoveable, always abounding in the work of the Lord, forasmuch as ye know that your labour is not in vain in the Lord. (1 Corinthians 15:58)

But exhort one another daily, while it is called To day; lest any of you be hardened through the deceitfulness of sin. For we are made partakers of Christ, if we hold the beginning of our confidence stedfast unto the end. (Hebrews 3:13-14)

KEEPING

To keep is to hold fast, preserve, and maintain. We stand fast and remain steadfast by keeping God's Word, keeping His ways, keeping His works, and keeping the faith.

But he said, Yea rather, blessed are they that hear the word of God, and keep it. (Luke 11:28)

Jesus answered and said unto him, If a man love me, he will keep my words: and my Father will love him, and we will come unto him, and make our abode with him. (John 14:23)

Now therefore hearken unto me, O ye children: for blessed are they that keep my ways. (Proverbs 8:32)

But that which ye have already hold fast till I come. And he that overcometh, and keepeth my works unto the end, to him will I give power over the nations. (Revelation 2:25-26)

CONTINUING

To continue is to stay, abide, remain, stand. We do not change. We do not depart from the faith. We do not fall away from the faith. We continue in the faith.

Then said Jesus to those Jews which believed on him, If ye continue in my word, then are ye my disciples indeed; And ye shall know the truth, and the truth shall make you free. (John 8:31-32)

But continue thou in the things which thou hast learned and hast been assured of, knowing of whom thou hast learned them. (2 Timothy 3:14)

And when they had preached the gospel to that city, and had taught many, they returned again to Lystra, and to Iconium, and Antioch, Confirming the souls of the disciples, and exhorting them to continue in the faith, and that we must through much tribulation enter into the kingdom of God. (Acts 14:21-22)

THE COST

There is a cost that comes with our faithfulness to God and His Word. The price we pay is having to endure the trials, tribulation, and persecution that comes with our faith.

> For which of you, intending to build a tower, sitteth not down first, and counteth the cost, whether he have sufficient to finish it? Lest haply, after he hath laid the foundation, and is not able to finish it, all that behold it begin to mock him, Saying, This man began to build, and was not able to finish it. (Luke 14:28-30)

ENDURING

To endure is to remain, to undergo, to bear trials. It is to have fortitude, to persevere, abide, take patiently, suffer.

> But he that shall endure unto the end, the same shall be saved. (Matthew 24:13)

> Behold, we count them happy which endure. (James 5:11)

> Wherefore seeing we also are compassed about with so great a cloud of witnesses, let us lay aside every weight, and the sin which doth so easily beset us, and let us run with patience the race that is set before us, Looking unto Jesus the author and finisher of our faith; who for the joy that was set before him endured the cross, despising the shame, and is set down at the right hand of the throne of God. (Hebrews 12:1-2)

Thanks to God's Word, we know what to expect and how to respond to whatever befalls us. Mercifully, we are given the assurance that with God's help we can endure even the most challenging and difficult trials and temptations.

WHAT TO EXPECT AND HOW TO RESPOND

1) EXPECT TROUBLE

Yet man is born unto trouble, as the sparks fly upward. (Job 5:7)

For nation shall rise against nation, and kingdom against kingdom: and there shall be earthquakes in divers places, and there shall be famines and troubles: these are the beginnings of sorrows. (Mark 13:8)

And at that time shall Michael stand up, the great prince which standeth for the children of thy people: and there shall be a time of trouble, such as never was since there was a nation even to that same time: and at that time thy people shall be delivered, every one that shall be found written in the book. (Daniel 12:1)

Biblical Response

God is our refuge and strength, a very present help in trouble. Therefore will not we fear, though the earth be removed, and though the mountains be carried into the midst of the sea; Though the waters thereof roar and be troubled, though the mountains shake with the swelling thereof. (Psalm 46:1-3)

In the day of my trouble I will call upon thee: for thou wilt answer me. (Psalm 86:7)

Let not your heart be troubled: ye believe in God, believe also in me. (John 14:1)

We are troubled on every side, yet not distressed; we are perplexed, but not in despair; Persecuted, but not forsaken; cast down, but not destroyed; Always bearing about in the body the dying of the Lord Jesus, that the life also of Jesus might be made manifest in our body. (2 Corinthians 4:8-10)

And ye shall hear of wars and rumours of wars: see that ye be not troubled: for all these things must come to pass, but the end is not yet. (Matthew 24:6)

Prayer

The troubles of my heart are enlarged: O bring thou me out of my distresses. (Psalm 25:17)

2) EXPECT SUFFERING

For unto you it is given in the behalf of Christ, not only to believe on him, but also to suffer for his sake. (Philippians 1:29)

For as the sufferings of Christ abound in us, so our consolation also aboundeth by Christ. (2 Corinthians 1:5)

Biblical Response

But rejoice, inasmuch as ye are partakers of Christ's sufferings; that, when his glory shall be revealed, ye may be glad also with exceeding joy. (1 Peter 4:13)

Yet if any man suffer as a Christian, let him not be ashamed; but let him glorify God on this behalf. (1 Peter 4:16)

And if children, then heirs; heirs of God, and joint-heirs with Christ; if so be that we suffer with him, that we may be also glorified together. For I reckon that the sufferings of this present time are not worthy to be compared with the glory which shall be revealed in us. (Romans 8:17-18)

And to him they agreed: and when they had called the apostles, and beaten them, they commanded that they should not speak in the name of Jesus, and let them go. And they departed from the presence of the council, rejoicing that they were counted worthy to suffer shame for his name. (Acts 5:40-41)

For this is thankworthy, if a man for conscience toward God endure grief, suffering wrongfully. For what glory is it, if, when ye be buffeted for your faults, ye shall take it patiently? but if, when ye do well, and suffer for it, ye take it patiently, this is acceptable with God. (1 Peter 2:19-20)

Prayer

Have mercy upon me, O LORD; consider my trouble which I suffer of them that hate me, thou that liftest me up from the gates of death. That I may show forth all thy praise in the gates of the daughter of Zion: I will rejoice in thy salvation. (Psalm 9:13-14)

3) EXPECT GRIEF AND SORROW

For in much wisdom is much grief: and he that increaseth knowledge increaseth sorrow. (Ecclesiastes 1:18)

For what hath man of all his labour, and of the vexation of his heart, wherein he hath laboured under the sun? For all his days are sorrows, and his travail grief; yea, his heart taketh not rest in the night. This is also vanity. (Ecclesiastes 2:22-23)

Biblical Response

Blessed are they that mourn: for they shall be comforted. (Matthew 5:4)

Sorrow is better than laughter: for by the sadness of the countenance the heart is made better. The heart of the wise is in the house of mourning; but the heart of fools is in the house of mirth. (Ecclesiastes 7:3-4)

As sorrowful, yet alway rejoicing as poor, yet making many rich; as having nothing, and yet possessing all things. (2 Corinthians 6:10)

For godly sorrow worketh repentance to salvation not to be repented of: but the sorrow of the world worketh death. (2 Corinthians 7:10)

Prayer

Have mercy upon me, O LORD, for I am in trouble: mine eye is consumed with grief, yea, my soul and my belly. (Psalm 31:9)

4) EXPECT PERSECUTION

Yea, and all that will live godly in Christ Jesus shall suffer persecution. (2 Timothy 3:12)

Remember the word that I said unto you, The servant is not greater than his lord. If they have persecuted me, they will also persecute you. (John 15:20)

Biblical Response

Blessed are they which are persecuted for righteousness' sake: for theirs is the kingdom of heaven. Blessed are ye, when men shall revile you, and persecute you, and shall say all manner of evil against you falsely, for my sake. Rejoice, and be exceeding glad: for great is your reward in heaven: for so persecuted they the prophets which were before you. (Matthew 5:10-12)

But I say unto you, Love your enemies, bless them that curse you, do good to them that hate you, and pray for them which despitefully use you, and persecute you. (Matthew 5:44)

Therefore I take pleasure in infirmities, in reproaches, in necessities, in persecutions, in distresses for Christ's sake: for when I am weak, then am I strong. (2 Corinthians 12:10)

Princes have persecuted me without a cause: but my heart standeth in awe of thy word. I rejoice at thy word, as one that findeth great spoil. (Psalm 119:161-162)

Prayer

O LORD my God, in thee do I put my trust: save me from all them that persecute me, and deliver me. (Psalm 7:1)

5) EXPECT AFFLICTION

Many are the afflictions of the righteous: but the LORD delivereth him out of them all. (Psalm 34:19)

That no man should be moved by these afflictions: for yourselves know that we are appointed thereunto. (1 Thessalonians 3:3)

For in those days shall be affliction, such as was not from the beginning of the creation which God created unto this time, neither shall be. (Mark 13:19)

Biblical Response

For which cause we faint not; but though our outward man perish, yet the inward man is renewed day by day. For our light affliction, which is but for a moment, worketh for us a far more exceeding and eternal weight of glory. (2 Corinthians 4:16-17)

This is my comfort in my affliction: for thy word hath quickened me. (Psalm 119:50)

It is good for me that I have been afflicted; that I might learn thy statutes. (Psalm 119:71)

Prayer

Turn thee unto me, and have mercy upon me; for I am desolate and afflicted. (Psalm 25:16)

6) EXPECT TRIBULATION

Confirming the souls of the disciples, and exhorting them to continue in the faith, and that we must through much tribulation enter into the kingdom of God. (Acts 14:22)

Biblical Response

When thou art in tribulation, and all these things are come upon thee, even in the latter days, if thou turn to the LORD thy God, and shalt be obedient unto his voice; (For the LORD thy God is a merciful God;) he will not forsake thee, neither destroy thee, nor forget the covenant of thy fathers which he sware unto them. (Deuteronomy 4:30-31)

These things I have spoken unto you, that in me ye might have peace. In the world ye shall have tribulation: but be of good cheer; I have overcome the world. (John 16:33)

Blessed be God, even the Father of our Lord Jesus Christ, the Father of mercies, and the God of all comfort; Who comforteth us in all our tribulation, that we may be able to comfort them which are in any trouble, by the comfort wherewith we ourselves are comforted of God. (2 Corinthians 1:3-4)

And not only so, but we glory in tribulations also: knowing that tribulation worketh patience; And patience, experience; and experience, hope. (Romans 5:3-4)

Great is my boldness of speech toward you, great is my glorying of you: I am filled with comfort, I am exceeding joyful in all our tribulation. (2 Corinthians 7:4)

Rejoicing in hope; patient in tribulation; continuing instant in prayer. (Romans 12:12)

Prayer

And, behold, as thy life was much set by this day in mine eyes, so let my life be much set by in the eyes of the LORD, and let him deliver me out of all tribulation. (1 Samuel 26:24)

7) EXPECT TEMPTATION

There hath no temptation taken you but such as is common to man: but God is faithful, who will not suffer you to be tempted above that ye are able; but will with the temptation also make a way to escape, that ye may be able to bear it. (1 Corinthians 10:13)

Because thou hast kept the word of my patience, I also will keep thee from the hour of temptation, which shall come upon all the world, to try them that dwell upon the earth. (Revelation 3:10)

Biblical Response

Watch and pray, that ye enter not into temptation: the spirit indeed is willing, but the flesh is weak. (Matthew 26:41)

My brethren, count it all joy when ye fall into divers temptations; Knowing this, that the trying of your faith worketh patience. (James 1:2-3)

Blessed is the man that endureth temptation: for when he is tried, he shall receive the crown of life, which the Lord hath promised to them that love him. (James 1:12)

Prayer

And lead us not into temptation, but deliver us from evil: For thine is the kingdom, and the power, and the glory, for ever. Amen. (Matthew 6:13)

8) EXPECT TRIALS

That the trial of your faith, being much more precious than of gold that perisheth, though it be tried with fire, might be found unto praise and honour and glory at the appearing of Jesus Christ: Whom having not seen, ye love; in whom, though now ye see him not, yet believing, ye rejoice with joy unspeakable and full of glory. (1 Peter 1:7-8)

Biblical Response

Beloved, think it not strange concerning the fiery trial which is to try you, as though some strange thing happened unto you: But rejoice, inasmuch as ye are partakers of Christ's sufferings; that, when his glory shall be revealed, ye may be glad also with exceeding joy. (1 Peter 4:12-13)

Prayer

O keep my soul, and deliver me: let me not be ashamed; for I put my trust in thee. (Psalm 25:20)

9) EXPECT HATRED

Marvel not, my brethren, if the world hate you. (1 John 3:13)

And ye shall be hated of all men for my name's sake. (Luke 21:17)

Then shall they deliver you up to be afflicted, and shall kill you: and ye shall be hated of all nations for my name's sake. (Matthew 24:9)

Biblical Response

Blessed are ye, when men shall hate you, and when they shall separate you from their company, and shall reproach you, and cast out your name as evil, for the Son of man's sake. Rejoice ye in that day, and leap for joy: for, behold, your reward is great in heaven: for in the like manner did their fathers unto the prophets. (Luke 6:22-23)

But I say unto you, Love your enemies, bless them that curse you, do good to them that hate you, and pray for them which despitefully use you, and persecute you. (Matthew 5:44)

Prayer

Deliver me out of the mire, and let me not sink: let me be delivered from them that hate me, and out of the deep waters. (Psalm 69:14)

10) EXPECT TO BE CALLED BEELZEBUB/SATAN

It is enough for the disciple that he be as his master, and the servant as his lord. If they have called the master of the house Beelzebub, how much more shall they call them of his household? (Matthew 10:25)

Biblical Response

Blessed are ye, when men shall revile you, and persecute you, and shall say all manner of evil against you falsely, for my sake. Rejoice, and be exceeding glad: for great is your reward in heaven: for so persecuted they the prophets which were before you. (Matthew 5:11-12)

Bless them which persecute you: bless, and curse not. (Romans 12:14)

And labour, working with our own hands: being reviled, we bless; being persecuted, we suffer it: Being defamed, we entreat: we are made as the filth of the world, and are the offscouring of all things unto this day. (1 Corinthians 4:12-13)

Prayer

My times are in thy hand: deliver me from the hand of mine enemies, and from them that persecute me. (Psalm 31:15)

11) EXPECT YOU MAY DIE FOR YOUR FAITH

Yea, for thy sake are we killed all the day long; we are counted as sheep for the slaughter. (Psalm 44:22)

These things have I spoken unto you, that ye should not be offended. They shall put you out of the synagogues: yea, the time cometh, that whosoever killeth you will think that he doeth God service. (John 16:1-2)

Then shall they deliver you up to be afflicted, and shall kill you: and ye shall be hated of all nations for my name's sake. (Matthew 24:9)

Biblical Response

And fear not them which kill the body, but are not able to kill the soul: but rather fear him which is able to destroy both soul and body in hell. (Matthew 10:28)

Fear none of those things which thou shalt suffer...be thou faithful unto death, and I will give thee a crown of life. (Revelation 2:10)

Precious in the sight of the LORD is the death of his saints. (Psalm 116:15)

For this God is our God for ever and ever: he will be our guide even unto death. (Psalm 48:14)

And they overcame him by the blood of the Lamb, and by the word of their testimony; and they loved not their lives unto the death. (Revelation 12:11)

Prayer

Yea, though I walk through the valley of the shadow of death, I will fear no evil: for thou art with me; thy rod and thy staff they comfort me. (Psalm 23:4)

12) EXPECT TO SEE JESUS

Looking for that blessed hope, and the glorious appearing of the great God and our Saviour Jesus Christ. (Titus 2:13)

Behold, he cometh with clouds; and every eye shall see him, and they also which pierced him: and all kindreds of the earth shall wail because of him. Even so, Amen. (Revelation 1:7)

For as the lightning cometh out of the east, and shineth even unto the west; so shall also the coming of the Son of man be. (Matthew 24:27)

Biblical Response

Blessed are those servants, whom the lord when he cometh shall find watching. (Luke 12:37)

And there shall be signs in the sun, and in the moon, and in the stars; and upon the earth distress of nations, with perplexity; the sea and the waves roaring; Men's hearts failing them for fear, and for looking after those things which are coming on the earth: for the powers of heaven shall be shaken. And then shall they see the Son of man coming in a cloud with power and great glory. And when these things begin to come to pass, then look up, and lift up your heads; for your redemption draweth nigh. (Luke 21:25-28)

For the Lord himself shall descend from heaven with a shout, with the voice of the archangel, and with the trump of God: and the dead in Christ shall rise first: Then we which are alive and remain shall be caught up together with them in the clouds, to meet the Lord in the air: and so shall we ever be with the Lord. Wherefore comfort one another with these words. (1 Thessalonians 4:16-18)

Be ye therefore ready also: for the Son of man cometh at an hour when ye think not. (Luke 12:40)

Prayer

He which testifieth these things saith, Surely I come quickly. Amen. Even so, come, Lord Jesus. (Revelation 22:20)

13) EXPECT A NEW HEAVEN AND A NEW EARTH

And I saw a new heaven and a new earth: for the first heaven and the first earth were passed away; and there was no more sea. And I John saw the holy city, new Jerusalem, coming down from God out of heaven, prepared as a bride adorned for her husband. (Revelation 21:1-2)

Biblical Response

He that overcometh shall inherit all things; and I will be his God, and he shall be my son. (Revelation 21:7)

CONCLUSION

Life can be extremely difficult and challenging. It is not easy being a biblical Christian. If we continue in His Word and remain steadfast in our faith, we are promised trials and tribulation. We know that we will be mocked, hated, betrayed, persecuted, and maybe even killed for our faith. But we are not to be deterred by a world and an apostate church that would seek to undo our testimony. Even in our most trying moments, we are encouraged to rejoice and be thankful as we glorify God and exhort one another daily to be steadfast in our faith until the very end:

Rejoice evermore. (1 Thessalonians 5:16)

In every thing give thanks: for this is the will of God in Christ Jesus concerning you. (1 Thessalonians 5:18)

I will praise thee, O Lord my God, with all my heart: and I will glorify thy name for evermore. (Psalm 86:12)

But exhort one another daily, while it is called To day; lest any of you be hardened through the deceitfulness of sin. For we are made partakers of Christ, if we hold the beginning of our confidence stedfast unto the end. (Hebrews 3:13-14)

Overcomer

To overcome is to subdue, conquer, prevail, to get the victory. Overcomers do not fall away. We are to be more than conquerors—we are to be overcomers. Paul said:

Nay, in all these things we are more than conquerors through him that loved us. For I am persuaded, that neither death, nor life, nor angels, nor principalities, nor powers, nor things present, nor things to come, Nor height, nor depth, nor any other creature, shall be able to separate us from the love of God, which is in Christ Jesus our Lord. (Romans 8:37-39)

Jesus said:

To him that overcometh will I grant to sit with me in my throne, even as I also overcame, and am set down with my Father in his throne. (Revelation 3:21)

Charge

With spiritual darkness coming on fast, we must share God's Word and work while we can.

I must work the works of him that sent me, while it is day: the night cometh, when no man can work. (John 9:4)

Brethren, I count not myself to have apprehended: but this one thing I do, forgetting those things which are behind, and reaching forth unto those things which are before, I press toward the mark for the prize of the high calling of God in Christ Jesus. (Philippians 3:13-14)

Encouragement

When we grow weary and faint, we must remember that our strength comes from the Lord. He will renew us for the task at hand. His grace is sufficient, and He perfects His strength in our weakness. As we are strengthened and encouraged, we must encourage others that God's Word is true and that His truth will prevail in the end. Evil will be vanquished, and those that are planted in the house of the Lord will flourish in the courts of our God.

And he said unto me, My grace is sufficient for thee: for my strength is made perfect in weakness. Most gladly therefore will I rather glory in my infirmities, that the power of Christ may rest upon me. (2 Corinthians 12:9)

Hast thou not known? hast thou not heard, that the everlasting God, the LORD, the Creator of the ends of the earth, fainteth not, neither is weary? there is no searching of his understanding. He giveth power to the faint; and to them that have no might he increaseth strength. Even the youths shall faint and be weary, and the young men shall utterly fall: But they that wait upon the LORD shall renew their strength; they shall mount up with wings as eagles; they shall run, and not be weary; and they shall walk, and not faint. (Isaiah 40:28-31)

When the wicked spring as the grass, and when all the workers of iniquity do flourish; it is that they shall be destroyed for ever: But thou, LORD, art most high for evermore. For, lo, thine enemies, O LORD, for, lo, thine enemies shall perish; all the workers of iniquity shall be scattered. . . . Mine eye also shall see my desire on mine enemies, and mine ears shall hear my desire of the wicked that rise up against me. The righteous shall flourish like the palm tree: he shall grow like a cedar in Lebanon. Those that be planted in the house of the LORD shall flourish in the courts of our God. (Psalm 92:7-9, 11-13)

CHAPTER ELEVEN

PATIENTLY WAITING AND ENDURING THROUGH IT ALL

For we are saved by hope: but hope that is seen is not hope: for what a man seeth, why doth he yet hope for? But if we hope for that we see not, then do we with patience wait for it. (Romans 8:24-25)

ENDURING PATIENCE

Webster's New World Dictionary defines the word "patient" as "bearing or enduring pain, trouble, etc. without complaining or losing self-control, calmly tolerating delay, confusion; able to wait calmly for something desired; steady, diligent, persevering." The Greek meaning according to *Strong's Concordance* is to have "a cheerful or hopeful endurance; a constancy or enduring patience; a patient continuance (waiting)." In short, patience may be seen as the ability to cheerfully and hopefully wait and endure—without complaint—whatever befalls us.

THE ISRAELITES' IMPATIENCE

The Bible makes it clear that Jesus' followers are to wait patiently for His return. In the Book of Exodus, the Bible records how the Israelites did not wait patiently when Moses "delayed" his return from Mount Sinai.

> And when the people saw that Moses delayed to come down out of the mount, the people gathered themselves together unto Aaron, and said unto him, Up, make us gods, which shall go before us; for as for this Moses, the man that brought us up out of the land of Egypt, we wot not what is become of him. (Exodus 32:1)

In their impatience the Israelites "corrupted themselves" by worshiping a god of their own making. Instead of waiting patiently for Moses and the true God of Israel, the people created another god. Scripture records how "the people sat down to eat and to drink, and rose up to play."

> And Aaron said unto them, Break off the golden earrings, which are in the ears of your wives, of your sons, and of your daughters, and bring them unto me. And all the people brake off the golden earrings which were in their ears, and brought them unto Aaron. And he received them at their hand, and fashioned it with a graving tool, after he had made it a molten calf: and they said, These be thy gods, O Israel, which brought thee up out of the land of Egypt. And when Aaron saw it, he built an altar before it; and Aaron made proclamation, and said, To morrow is a feast to the LORD. And they rose up early on the morrow, and offered burnt offerings, and brought peace offerings; and the people sat down to eat and to drink, and rose up to play. And the LORD said unto Moses, Go, get thee down; for thy people, which thou broughtest out of the land of Egypt, have corrupted themselves. (Exodus 32:2-7)

The apostle Paul cites this particular incident to warn how the Israelites' simple act of impatience resulted in their "corrupting themselves":

> Neither be ye idolaters, as were some of them; as it is written, The people sat down to eat and drink, and rose up to play . . . Now all these things happened unto them for ensamples: and they are written for our admonition, upon whom the ends of the

world are come. Wherefore let him that thinketh he standeth take heed lest he fall. (1 Corinthians 10:7,11-12)

In a letter to the Romans, Paul emphasizes how these former events described in Scripture can comfort us and help us to learn patience and hope.

For whatsoever things were written aforetime were written for our learning, that we through patience and comfort of the scriptures might have hope. (Romans 15:4)

The first stanza of the hymn *My Soul With Patience Waits* underscores the importance of patience and the comfort of God's Word—how we are to patiently wait for our Lord:

My soul with patience waits
For Thee, the living Lord
My hopes are on thy promise built,
Thy never-failing word.

The following selected verses from Scripture describe the importance of patience and how—with God's help—we are to patiently wait and endure whatever circumstances arise in our lives.

PATIENCE

GOD IS THE GOD OF PATIENCE

Now the God of patience and consolation grant you to be likeminded one toward another according to Christ Jesus: That ye may with one mind and one mouth glorify God, even the Father of our Lord Jesus Christ. (Romans 15:5-6)

ADD PATIENCE TO YOUR FAITH

Whereby are given unto us exceeding great and precious promises: that by these ye might be partakers of the divine nature, having escaped the corruption that is in the world through lust. And beside this, giving all diligence, add to your faith virtue; and to virtue knowledge; And to knowledge temperance; and to temperance patience; and to patience godliness; And to godliness brotherly kindness; and to brotherly kindness charity. For if these things be in you, and abound, they make you that ye shall neither be barren nor unfruitful in the knowledge of our Lord Jesus Christ. (2 Peter 1:4-8)

THROUGH PATIENCE WE HAVE HOPE

For whatsoever things were written aforetime were written for our learning, that we through patience and comfort of the scriptures might have hope. (Romans 15:4)

FOLLOW AFTER PATIENCE

But thou, O man of God, flee these things; and follow after righteousness, godliness, faith, love, patience, meekness. (1 Timothy 6:11)

RUN WITH PATIENCE

Wherefore seeing we also are compassed about with so great a cloud of witnesses, let us lay aside every weight, and the sin which doth so easily beset us, and let us run with patience the race that is set before us, Looking unto Jesus the author and finisher of our faith; who for the joy that was set before him endured the cross, despising the shame, and is set down at the right hand of the throne of God. (Hebrews 12:1-2)

PATIENCE BRINGS FORTH FRUIT

But that on the good ground are they, which in an honest and good heart, having heard the word, keep it, and bring forth fruit with patience. (Luke 8:15)

TEMPTATIONS WORKETH PATIENCE

My brethren, count it all joy when ye fall into divers temptations; Knowing this, that the trying of your faith worketh patience. But let patience have her perfect work, that ye may be perfect and entire, wanting nothing. (James 1:2-4)

PATIENCE AND FAITH IN THE MIDST OF PERSECUTIONS AND TRIBULATIONS

So that we ourselves glory in you in the churches of God for your patience and faith in all your persecutions and tribulations that ye endure: Which is a manifest token of the righteous judgment of God, that ye may be counted worthy of the kingdom of God, for which ye also suffer. (2 Thessalonians 1:4-5)

TRIBULATION PRODUCES PATIENCE

And not only so, but we glory in tribulations also: knowing that tribulation worketh patience; And patience, experience; and experience, hope: And hope maketh not ashamed; because the love of God is shed abroad in our hearts by the Holy Ghost which is given unto us. (Romans 5:3-5)

PATIENCE IN ALL THINGS

But in all things approving ourselves as the ministers of God, in much patience, in afflictions, in necessities, in distresses, In stripes, in imprisonments, in tumults, in labours, in watchings, in fastings. (2 Corinthians 6:4-5)

THROUGH FAITH AND PATIENCE WE INHERIT THE PROMISES

And we desire that every one of you do show the same diligence to the full assurance of hope unto the end: That ye be not slothful, but followers of them who through faith and patience inherit the promises. (Hebrews 6:11-12)

For ye have need of patience, that, after ye have done the will of God, ye might receive the promise. (Hebrews 10:36)

THE PATIENCE OF JOB

Behold, we count them happy which endure. Ye have heard of the patience of Job, and have seen the end of the Lord; that the Lord is very pitiful, and of tender mercy. (James 5:11)

THE PATIENCE OF PAUL

But thou hast fully known my doctrine, manner of life, purpose, faith, longsuffering, charity, patience, Persecutions, afflictions, which came unto me at Antioch, at Iconium, at Lystra; what persecutions I endured: but out of them all the Lord delivered me. (2 Timothy 3:10-11)

THE PATIENCE OF THE PROPHETS

Take, my brethren, the prophets, who have spoken in the name of the Lord, for an example of suffering affliction, and of patience. Behold, we count them happy which endure. Ye have heard of the patience of Job, and have seen the end of the Lord; that the Lord is very pitiful, and of tender mercy. (James 5:10-11)

THE PATIENCE OF JESUS CHRIST

I John, who also am your brother, and companion in tribulation, and in the kingdom and patience of Jesus Christ, was in the isle that is called Patmos, for the word of God, and for the testimony of Jesus Christ. (Revelation 1:9)

THE PATIENCE OF THE CHURCH IN EPHESUS

I know thy works, and thy labour, and thy patience, and how thou canst not bear them which are evil: and thou hast tried them which say they are apostles, and are not, and hast found them liars: And hast borne, and hast patience, and for my name's sake hast laboured, and hast not fainted. (Revelation 2:-2-3)

THE PATIENCE OF THE CHURCH IN THYATIRA

I know thy works, and charity, and service, and faith, and thy patience, and thy works; and the last to be more than the first. (Revelation 2:19)

THE PATIENCE OF THE CHURCH IN PHILADELPHIA

Because thou hast kept the word of my patience, I also will keep thee from the hour of temptation, which shall come upon all the world, to try them that dwell upon the earth. Behold, I come quickly: hold that fast which thou hast, that no man take thy crown. (Revelation 3:10-11)

THE PATIENCE OF THE SAINTS

Here is the patience of the saints: here are they that keep the commandments of God, and the faith of Jesus. (Revelation 14:12)

He that leadeth into captivity shall go into captivity: he that killeth with the sword must be killed with the sword. Here is the patience and the faith of the saints. (Revelation 13:10)

And the servant of the Lord must not strive; but be gentle unto all men, apt to teach, patient. (2 Timothy 2:24)

OUR PATIENCE OF HOPE IS IN THE LORD JESUS

We give thanks to God always for you all, making mention of you in our prayers; Remembering without ceasing your work of faith, and labour of love, and patience of hope in our Lord Jesus Christ, in the sight of God and our Father; Knowing, brethren beloved, your election of God. (1 Thessalonians 1:2-4)

ENCOURAGEMENT FOR THOSE WHO ARE PATIENT

In your patience possess ye your souls. (Luke 21:19)

PRAYER

For this cause we also, since the day we heard it, do not cease to pray for you, and to desire that ye might be filled with the knowledge of his will in all wisdom and spiritual understanding; That ye might walk worthy of the Lord unto all pleasing, being fruitful in every good work, and increasing in the knowledge of God; Strengthened with all might, according to his glorious power, unto all patience and longsuffering with joyfulness. (Colossians 1:9-11)

WAITING

OUR EYES WAIT UPON THE LORD

Unto thee lift I up mine eyes, O thou that dwellest in the heavens. Behold, as the eyes of servants look unto the hand of their masters, and as the eyes of a maiden unto the hand of her mistress; so our eyes wait upon the LORD our God, until that he have mercy upon us. (Psalm 123:1-2)

The LORD upholdeth all that fall, and raiseth up all those that be bowed down. The eyes of all wait upon thee; and thou givest them their meat in due season. (Psalm 145:14-15)

OUR SOULS WAIT UPON THE LORD

I wait for the LORD, my soul doth wait, and in his word do I hope. My soul waiteth for the Lord more than they that watch for the morning: I say, more than they that watch for the morning. (Psalm 130:5-6)

WAIT FOR THE GOD OF OUR SALVATION

Trust ye not in a friend, put ye not confidence in a guide: keep the doors of thy mouth from her that lieth in thy bosom. For the son dishonoureth the father, the daughter riseth up against her mother, the daughter in law against her mother in law; a man's enemies are the men of his own house. Therefore I will look unto the LORD; I will wait for the God of my salvation: my God will hear me. (Micah 7:5-7)

And it shall be said in that day, Lo, this is our God; we have waited for him, and he will save us: this is the LORD; we have waited for him, we will be glad and rejoice in his salvation. (Isaiah 25:9)

The LORD is good unto them that wait for him, to the soul that seeketh him. It is good that a man should both hope and quietly wait for the salvation of the LORD. (Lamentations 3:25-26)

Truly my soul waiteth upon God: from him cometh my salvation. He only is my rock and my salvation; he is my defence; I shall not be greatly moved. (Psalm 62:1-2)

Say not thou, I will recompense evil; but wait on the LORD, and he shall save thee. (Proverbs 20:22)

WAIT PATIENTLY FOR THE LORD

Rest in the LORD, and wait patiently for him: fret not thyself because of him who prospereth in his way, because of the man who bringeth wicked devices to pass. (Psalm 37:7)

I waited patiently for the LORD; and he inclined unto me, and heard my cry. He brought me up also out of an horrible pit, out of the miry clay, and set my feet upon a rock, and established my goings. And he hath put a new song in my mouth, even praise unto our God: many shall see it, and fear, and shall trust in the LORD. Blessed is that man that maketh the LORD his trust, and respecteth not the proud, nor such as turn aside to lies. (Psalm 40:1-4)

But the Lord is faithful, who shall stablish you, and keep you from evil. And we have confidence in the Lord touching you, that ye both do and will do the things which we command you.

And the Lord direct your hearts into the love of God, and into the patient waiting for Christ. (2 Thessalonians 3:3-5)

WAIT ON HIS NAME

I will praise thee for ever, because thou hast done it: and I will wait on thy name; for it is good before thy saints. (Psalm 52:9)

WAIT FOR THE LORD WHO IS OUR HOPE

And now, Lord, what wait I for? my hope is in thee. (Psalm 39:7)

WAIT ON THE LORD WHO IS OUR HELP

Our soul waiteth for the LORD: he is our help and our shield. (Psalm 33:20)

WAIT ONLY ON HIM

My soul, wait thou only upon God; for my expectation is from him. He only is my rock and my salvation: he is my defence; I shall not be moved. (Psalm 62:5-6)

WAIT FOR THE LORD IN TIMES OF TROUBLE

O LORD, be gracious unto us; we have waited for thee: be thou their arm every morning, our salvation also in the time of trouble. (Isaiah 33:2)

I sink in deep mire, where there is no standing: I am come into deep waters, where the floods overflow me. I am weary of my crying: my throat is dried: mine eyes fail while I wait for my God. (Psalm 69:2-3)

WAIT ON THE LORD TO RENEW OUR STRENGTH

Hast thou not known? hast thou not heard, that the everlasting God, the LORD, the Creator of the ends of the earth, fainteth not, neither is weary? there is no searching of his understanding. He giveth power to the faint; and to them that have no might he increaseth strength. Even the youths shall faint and be weary, and the young men shall utterly fall: But they that wait upon the LORD shall renew their strength; they shall mount up with wings as eagles; they shall run, and not be weary; and they shall walk, and not faint. (Isaiah 40:28-31)

WAIT ON THE LORD ALL DAY

Show me thy ways, O LORD; teach me thy paths. Lead me in thy truth, and teach me: for thou art the God of my salvation; on thee do I wait all the day. (Psalm 25:4-5)

WAIT ON GOD CONTINUALLY

Therefore turn thou to thy God: keep mercy and judgment, and wait on thy God continually. (Hosea 12:6)

WAIT ON THE LORD FROM HEAVEN

For they themselves show of us what manner of entering in we had unto you, and how ye turned to God from idols to serve the living and true God; And to wait for his Son from heaven, whom he raised from the dead, even Jesus, which delivered us from the wrath to come. (1 Thessalonians 1:9-10)

Let your loins be girded about, and your lights burning; And ye yourselves like unto men that wait for their lord, when he will return from the wedding; that when he cometh and knocketh, they may open unto him immediately. (Luke 12:35-36)

WAIT ON THE LORD FOR REDEMPTION

For we know that the whole creation groaneth and travaileth in pain together until now. And not only they, but ourselves also, which have the firstfruits of the Spirit, even we ourselves groan within ourselves, waiting for the adoption, to wit, the redemption of our body. (Romans 8:22-23)

WAIT ON THE LORD TO BE CONFIRMED BLAMELESS

So that ye come behind in no gift; waiting for the coming of our Lord Jesus Christ: Who shall also confirm you unto the end, that ye may be blameless in the day of our Lord Jesus Christ. (1 Corinthians 1:7-8)

WAIT ON THE LORD AND INHERIT THE EARTH

For evildoers shall be cut off: but those that wait upon the LORD, they shall inherit the earth. (Psalm 37:9)

Wait on the LORD, and keep his way, and he shall exalt thee to inherit the land: when the wicked are cut off, thou shalt see it. (Psalm 37:34)

BLESSED ARE THOSE WHO WAIT FOR THE LORD

And therefore will the LORD wait, that he may be gracious unto you, and therefore will he be exalted, that he may have mercy upon you: for the LORD is a God of judgment: blessed are all they that wait for him. (Isaiah 30:18)

Many shall be purified, and made white, and tried; but the wicked shall do wickedly: and none of the wicked shall understand; but the wise shall understand. And from the time that the daily sacrifice shall be taken away, and the abomination that maketh desolate set up, there shall be a thousand two hundred and ninety days. Blessed is he that waiteth, and cometh to the thousand three hundred and five and thirty days. But go thou thy way till the end be: for thou shalt rest, and stand in thy lot at the end of the days. (Daniel 12:10-13)

ENCOURAGEMENT FOR THOSE WHO WAIT

For since the beginning of the world men have not heard, nor perceived by the ear, neither hath the eye seen, O God, beside thee, what he hath prepared for him that waiteth for him. (Isaiah 64:4)

PRAYER

The troubles of my heart are enlarged: O bring thou me out of my distresses. Look upon mine affliction and my pain; and forgive all my sins. Consider mine enemies; for they are many; and they hate me with cruel hatred. O keep my soul, and deliver me: let me not be ashamed; for I put my trust in thee. Let integrity and uprightness preserve me; for I wait on thee. (Psalm 25:17-21)

ENDURING

JESUS ENDURED THE CROSS

Looking unto Jesus the author and finisher of our faith; who for the joy that was set before him endured the cross, despising the shame, and is set down at the right hand of the throne of God. For consider him that endured such contradiction of sinners against himself, lest ye be wearied and faint in your minds. (Hebrews 12:2-3)

ENDURE TEMPTATION

Blessed is the man that endureth temptation: for when he is tried, he shall receive the crown of life, which the Lord hath promised to them that love him. (James 1:12)

ENDURE CHASTENING

For whom the Lord loveth he chasteneth, and scourgeth every son whom he receiveth. If ye endure chastening, God dealeth with you as with sons; for what son is he whom the father chasteneth not? (Hebrews 12:6-7)

ENDURE HARDNESS

Thou therefore endure hardness, as a good soldier of Jesus Christ. (2 Timothy 2:3)

ENDURE AFFLICTION

But watch thou in all things, endure afflictions, do the work of an evangelist, make full proof of thy ministry. (2 Timothy 4:5)

ENDURE SUFFERING

And whether we be afflicted, it is for your consolation and salvation, which is effectual in the enduring of the same sufferings which we also suffer: or whether we be comforted, it is for your consolation and salvation. (2 Corinthians 1:6)

For this is thankworthy, if a man for conscience toward God endure grief, suffering wrongfully. For what glory is it, if, when ye be buffeted for your faults, ye shall take it patiently? but if, when ye do well, and suffer for it, ye take it patiently, this is acceptable with God. (1 Peter 2:19-20)

ENDURE PERSECUTIONS, TRIBULATIONS

So that we ourselves glory in you in the churches of God for your patience and faith in all your persecutions and tribulations that ye endure: Which is a manifest token of the righteous judgment of God, that ye may be counted worthy of the kingdom of God, for which ye also suffer: (2 Thessalonians 1:4-5)

ENDURE ALL THINGS

Therefore I endure all things for the elect's sakes, that they may also obtain the salvation which is in Christ Jesus with eternal glory. (2 Timothy 2:10)

ENDURE TO THE END

Then shall they deliver you up to be afflicted, and shall kill you: and ye shall be hated of all nations for my name's sake. And then shall many be offended, and shall betray one another, and shall hate one another. And many false prophets shall rise, and shall deceive many. And because iniquity shall abound, the love of many shall wax cold. But he that shall endure unto the end, the same shall be saved. (Matthew 24:9-13)

ENCOURAGEMENT FOR THOSE WHO ENDURE

Behold, we count them happy which endure. (James 5:11)

PRAYER

Charity suffereth long, and is kind; charity envieth not; charity vaunteth not itself, is not puffed up, Doth not behave itself unseemly, seeketh not her own, is not easily provoked, thinketh no evil; Rejoiceth not in iniquity, but rejoiceth in the truth; Beareth all things, believeth all things, hopeth all things, endureth all things. (1 Corinthians 13:4-7)

CHAPTER TWELVE

GOD'S WORD
THROUGH IT ALL

Several years ago I was at a church conference in Olathe, Kansas. In the middle of citing a verse from the book of Jeremiah, the speaker suddenly looked up from the text with a huge smile on his face. Looking out at us, he joyfully exclaimed—"I love the Bible!" I immediately and enthusiastically agreed. What an amazing book! It tells us the truth, the whole truth, and nothing but the truth. While it lifts us up and shows us the way to salvation, it tells us who Jesus is, and it tells us who He is not. God's true authentic Word—we would be totally lost without it. However in today's compromised church, spiritual experience seems to be the name of the game. Consequently, there seems to be more interest in a word from God rather than in the Word of God. Lest we become compromised ourselves, we must never take God's Word for granted. What a gift, what a treasure, what a wonder the Holy Bible is. It truly is the Word of God as it inspires, nurtures, guides, and sustains us in our walk with the Lord. God's Word is awesome—so awesome, in fact, that God magnifies His Word above everything else (Psalm 138:2). And when one reads through the Scriptures to see what the Bible says about the Bible, it is an amazing thing to behold. The following verses are just some of what God's Word says about God's Word.

GOD'S WORD

GOD'S WORD IS THE WORD OF GOD

For this cause also thank we God without ceasing, because, when ye received the word of God which ye heard of us, ye received it not as the word of men, but as it is in truth, the word of God, which effectually worketh also in you that believe. (1 Thessalonians 2:13)

GOD'S WORD IS MAGNIFIED BY GOD ABOVE HIS OWN NAME

I will worship toward thy holy temple, and praise thy name for thy lovingkindness and for thy truth: for thou hast magnified thy word above all thy name. (Psalm 138:2)

GOD'S WORD IS GOOD

For it is impossible for those who were once enlightened, and have tasted of the heavenly gift, and were made partakers of the Holy Ghost, And have tasted the good word of God, and the powers of the world to come, If they shall fall away, to renew them again unto repentance; seeing they crucify to themselves the Son of God afresh, and put him to an open shame. (Hebrews 6:4-6)

GOD'S WORD IS RIGHT

For the word of the LORD is right; and all his works are done in truth. (Psalm 33:4)

GOD'S WORD IS AWESOME

Princes have persecuted me without a cause: but my heart standeth in awe of thy word. (Psalm 119:161)

GOD'S WORD IS INSPIRED

All scripture is given by inspiration of God, and is profitable for doctrine, for reproof, for correction, for instruction in righteousness: That the man of God may be perfect, thoroughly furnished unto all good works. (2 Timothy 3:16-17)

GOD'S WORD IS SURE

The LORD on high is mightier than the noise of many waters, yea, than the mighty waves of the sea. Thy testimonies are very sure: holiness becometh thine house, O LORD, for ever. (Psalm 93:4-5)

GOD'S WORD IS PURE

The words of the LORD are pure words: as silver tried in a furnace of earth, purified seven times. (Psalm 12:6)

Thy word is very pure: therefore thy servant loveth it. (Psalm 119:140)

Every word of God is pure: he is a shield unto them that put their trust in him. (Proverbs 30:5)

GOD'S WORD IS TRIED

As for God, his way is perfect: the word of the LORD is tried: he is a buckler to all those that trust in him. (Psalm 18:30)

GOD'S WORD IS TRUE

Thy word is true from the beginning: and every one of thy righteous judgments endureth for ever. (Psalm 119:160)

GOD'S WORD IS TRUTH

Sanctify them through thy truth: thy word is truth. (John 17:17)

GOD'S WORD IS PRECIOUS

Whereby are given unto us exceeding great and precious promises: that by these ye might be partakers of the divine nature, having escaped the corruption that is in the world through lust. (2 Peter 1:4)

GOD'S WORD IS SWEET

How sweet are thy words unto my taste! yea, sweeter than honey to my mouth! (Psalm 119:103)

GOD'S WORD IS WONDERFUL

Thy testimonies are wonderful: therefore doth my soul keep them. (Psalm 119:129)

GOD'S WORD IS OUR SONG

Thy statutes have been my songs in the house of my pilgrimage. (Psalm 119:54)

GOD'S WORD IS OUR JOY

Thy words were found, and I did eat them; and thy word was unto me the joy and rejoicing of mine heart: for I am called by thy name, O LORD God of hosts. (Jeremiah 15:16)

GOD'S WORD IS OUR DELIGHT

Unless thy law had been my delights, I should then have perished in mine affliction. (Psalm 119:92)

GOD'S WORD IS POWERFUL

For the word of God is quick, and powerful, and sharper than any twoedged sword piercing even to the dividing asunder of soul and spirit, and of the joints and marrow, and is a discerner of the thoughts and intents of the heart. (Hebrews 4:12)

GOD'S WORD IS LIGHT

The entrance of thy words giveth light; it giveth understanding unto the simple. (Psalm 119:130)

Thy word is a lamp unto my feet, and a light unto my path. (Psalm 119:105)

GOD'S WORD WILL MAKE YOU WISE

And that from a child thou hast known the holy scriptures, which are able to make thee wise unto salvation through faith which is in Christ Jesus. (2 Timothy 3:15)

GOD'S WORD QUICKENS

I am afflicted very much: quicken me, O LORD, according unto thy word. (Psalm 119:107)

This is my comfort in my affliction: for thy word hath quickened me. (Psalm 119:50)

GOD'S WORD IS LIKE FIRE

Is not my word like as a fire? saith the LORD; and like a hammer that breaketh the rock in pieces? (Jeremiah 23:29)

GOD'S WORD CLEANSES

Wherewithal shall a young man cleanse his way? by taking heed thereto according to thy word. (Psalm 119:9)

GOD'S WORD UPHOLDS

Uphold me according unto thy word, that I may live: and let me not be ashamed of my hope. (Psalm 119:116)

GOD'S WORD GIVES US UNDERSTANDING

Through thy precepts I get understanding: therefore I hate every false way. (Psalm 119:104)

GOD'S WORD DELIVERS

Let my supplication come before thee: deliver me according to thy word. (Psalm 119:170)

GOD'S WORD IS OUR COUNSELOR

Thy testimonies also are my delight and my counsellors. (Psalm 119:24)

GOD'S WORD IS NOT BOUND

Wherein I suffer trouble, as an evil doer, even unto bonds; but the word of God is not bound. (2 Timothy 2:9)

GOD'S WORD WILL NOT RETURN VOID

So shall my word be that goeth forth out of my mouth: it shall not return unto me void, but it shall accomplish that which I please, and it shall prosper in the thing whereto I sent it. (Isaiah 55:11)

GOD'S WORD IS EVERLASTING

The righteousness of thy testimonies is everlasting: give me understanding, and I shall live. (Psalm 119:144)

WHAT IS OUR RESPONSE TO GOD'S WORD?

WE ARE TO TREMBLE AT GOD'S WORD

For all those things hath mine hand made, and all those things have been, saith the LORD: but to this man will I look, even to him that is poor and of a contrite spirit, and trembleth at my word. (Isaiah 66:2)

Hear the word of the LORD, ye that tremble at his word; Your brethren that hated you, that cast you out for my name's sake, said, Let the LORD be glorified: but he shall appear to your joy, and they shall be ashamed. (Isaiah 66:5)

WE ARE TO REJOICE IN GOD'S WORD

I rejoice at thy word, as one that findeth great spoil. (Psalm 119:162)

WE ARE TO PRAISE GOD'S WORD

In God I will praise his word, in God I have put my trust; I will not fear what flesh can do unto me. (Psalm 56:4)

In God will I praise his word: in the LORD will I praise his word. (Psalm 56:10)

WE ARE TO BE COMFORTED BY GOD'S WORD

For whatsoever things were written aforetime were written for our learning, that we through patience and comfort of the scriptures might have hope. (Romans 15:4)

WE ARE TO HOPE IN GOD'S WORD

Thou art my hiding place and my shield: I hope in thy word. (Psalm 119:114)

They that fear thee will be glad when they see me; because I have hoped in thy word. (Psalm 119:74)

My soul fainteth for thy salvation: but I hope in thy word. (Psalm 119:81)

I wait for the LORD, my soul doth wait, and in his word do I hope. (Palm 130:5)

WE ARE TO TRUST IN GOD'S WORD

So shall I have wherewith to answer him that reproacheth me: for I trust in thy word. (Psalm 119:42)

WE ARE TO DESIRE GOD'S WORD

As newborn babes, desire the sincere milk of the word, that ye may grow thereby. (1 Peter 2:2)

WE ARE TO STUDY GOD'S WORD

Study to show thyself approved unto God, a workman that needeth not to be ashamed, rightly dividing the word of truth. (2 Timothy 2:15)

WE ARE TO MEDITATE ON GOD'S WORD

O how love I thy law! it is my meditation all the day. (Psalm 119:97)

My hands also will I lift up unto thy commandments, which I have loved; and I will meditate in thy statutes. (Psalm 119:48)

I have more understanding than all my teachers: for thy testimonies are my meditation. (Psalm 119:99)

WE ARE TO LET THE WORD OF GOD DWELL IN US

Let the word of Christ dwell in you richly in all wisdom; teaching and admonishing one another in psalms and hymns and spiritual songs, singing with grace in your hearts to the Lord. (Colossians 3:16)

WE ARE TO LIVE BY THE WORD OF GOD

And he humbled thee, and suffered thee to hunger, and fed thee with manna, which thou knewest not, neither did thy fathers know; that he might make thee know that man doth not live by bread only, but by every word that proceedeth out of the mouth of the LORD doth man live. (Deuteronomy 8:3)

WE ARE TO ORDER OUR STEPS IN GOD'S WORD

Order my steps in thy word: and let not any iniquity have dominion over me. (Psalm 119:133)

WE ARE NOT TO CORRUPT THE WORD OF GOD

For we are not as many, which corrupt the word of God: but as of sincerity, but as of God, in the sight of God speak we in Christ. (2 Corinthians 2:17)

WE ARE NOT TO HANDLE THE WORD OF GOD DECEITFULLY

Therefore seeing we have this ministry, as we have received mercy, we faint not; But have renounced the hidden things of dishonesty, not walking in craftiness, nor handling the word of God deceitfully. (2 Corinthians 4:1-2)

WE ARE NOT TO ADD OR SUBTRACT FROM GOD'S WORD

What thing soever I command you, observe to do it: thou shalt not add thereto, nor diminish from it. (Deuteronomy 12:32)

Add thou not unto his words, lest he reprove thee, and thou be found a liar. (Proverbs 30:6)

WE ARE TO GLORIFY GOD'S WORD

And when the Gentiles heard this, they were glad, and glorified the word of the Lord: and as many as were ordained to eternal life believed. (Acts 13:48)

WE ARE TO GAIN OUR FAITH FROM HEARING GOD'S WORD

So then faith cometh by hearing, and hearing by the word of God. (Romans 10:17)

Verily, verily, I say unto you, He that heareth my word, and believeth on him that sent me, hath everlasting life, and shall not come into condemnation; but is passed from death unto life. (John 5:24)

WE ARE SAVED BY GOD'S WORD

Wherefore lay apart all filthiness and superfluity of naughtiness, and receive with meekness the engrafted word, which is able to save your souls. (James 1:21)

WE ARE TO BE DOERS OF GOD'S WORD

But be ye doers of the word, and not hearers only, deceiving your own selves. (James 1:22)

WE ARE TO HOLD FORTH THE WORD OF GOD

Holding forth the word of life; that I may rejoice in the day of Christ, that I have not run in vain, neither laboured in vain. (Philippians 2:16)

WE ARE TO PREACH GOD'S WORD

Preach the word; be instant in season, out of season; reprove, rebuke, exhort with all longsuffering and doctrine. (2 Timothy 4:2)

WE ARE TO CONTINUE IN GOD'S WORD

Then said Jesus to those Jews which believed on him, If ye continue in my word, then are ye my disciples indeed; and ye shall know the truth, and the truth shall make you free. (John 8:31-32)

WE ARE TO RESIST TEMPTATION BY GOD'S WORD

And when the tempter came to him, he said, If thou be the Son of God, command that these stones be made bread. But he answered and said, It is written, Man shall not live by bread alone, but by every word that proceedeth out of the mouth of God. (Matthew 4:3-4)

WE ARE NOT TO FORGET GOD'S WORD

I will delight myself in thy statutes: I will not forget thy word. (Psalm 119:16)

I am small and despised: yet do not I forget thy precepts. (Psalm 119:141)

WE ARE TO HIDE GOD'S WORD IN OUR HEART

Thy word have I hid in mine heart, that I might not sin against thee. (Psalm 119:11)

WE ARE TO KEEP GOD'S WORD

But whoso keepeth his word, in him verily is the love of God perfected: hereby know we that we are in him. (1 John 2:5)

Jesus answered and said unto him, If a man love me, he will keep my words: and my Father will love him, and we will come unto him, and make our abode with him. (John 14:23)

I know thy works: behold, I have set before thee an open door, and no man can shut it: for thou hast a little strength, and hast kept my word, and hast not denied my name. (Revelation 3:8)

But he said, Yea rather, blessed are they that hear the word of God, and keep it. (Luke 11:28)

Blessed are the undefiled in the way, who walk in the law of the LORD. Blessed are they that keep his testimonies, and that seek him with the whole heart. (Psalm 119:1-2)

My soul hath kept thy testimonies; and I love them exceedingly. (Psalm 119:167)

WE ARE TO STAND FAST IN GOD'S WORD

Therefore, brethren, stand fast, and hold the traditions which ye have been taught, whether by word, or our epistle. (2 Thessalonians 2:15)

WE ARE TO BATTLE USING GOD'S WORD

Above all, taking the shield of faith, wherewith ye shall be able to quench all the fiery darts of the wicked. And take the helmet of salvation, and the sword of the Spirit, which is the word of God. (Ephesians 6:16-17)

WE MAY BE SLAIN FOR THE WORD OF GOD

And when he had opened the fifth seal, I saw under the altar the souls of them that were slain for the word of God, and for the testimony which they held. (Revelation 6:9)

And I saw thrones, and they sat upon them, and judgment was given unto them: and I saw the souls of them that were beheaded for the witness of Jesus, and for the word of God, and which had not worshipped the beast, neither his image, neither had received his mark upon their foreheads, or in their hands; and they lived and reigned with Christ a thousand years. (Revelation 20:4)

GOD'S WORD STANDS FOREVER

For ever, O LORD, thy word is settled in heaven. (Psalm 119:89)

Concerning thy testimonies, I have known of old that thou hast founded them for ever. (Psalm 119:152)

The words of the LORD are pure words: as silver tried in a furnace of earth, purified seven times. Thou shalt keep them, O LORD, thou shalt preserve them from this generation for ever. (Psalm 12:6-7)

The grass withereth, the flower fadeth: but the word of our God shall stand for ever. (Isaiah 40:8)

Heaven and earth shall pass away, but my words shall not pass away. (Matthew 24:35)

A HOMELESS MAN & GOD'S WORD

Years ago, I directed a storefront ministry in Northern California that served the homeless mentally ill. One afternoon a young man came in and told me how he had recently been released from prison. He said he had noticed that men who had become born again Christians in prison were getting out of prison early. He said he wasn't stupid. He got himself a Bible, went to the Bible study, and feigned being born again. Sure enough, he got an early release. He told me that when he left the prison that last day, he hung his Bible on the prison's front gate and just walked away. He had outsmarted the system and was leaving prison and all that Bible stuff behind. But while he left his Bible hanging on the prison gate, he was surprised to find that the Word of God had been firmly planted within his heart. Recognizing that God's Word was active and alive in his life, he soon committed his life to the Lord. Now he truly was born again and only too happy to call himself a Christian.

GOD'S WORD IS AWESOME

Let all the earth fear the LORD: let all the inhabitants of the world stand in awe of him. For he spake, and it was done; he commanded, and it stood fast. The LORD bringeth the counsel of the heathen to nought: he maketh the devices of the people of none effect. The counsel of the LORD standeth for ever, the thoughts of his heart to all generations. Blessed is the nation whose God is the LORD; and the people whom he hath chosen for his own inheritance. (Psalm 33:8-12)

Princes have persecuted me without a cause: but my heart standeth in awe of thy word. (Psalm 119:161)

CHAPTER THIRTEEN

GOD'S BLESSINGS
THROUGH IT ALL

Anumber of traditional hymns speak of our many blessings in Christ. As previously mentioned, *Count Your Blessings* reminds us that even in our darkest moments we can rejoice and count our blessings:

> When upon life's billows you are tempest tossed,
> When you are discouraged, thinking all is lost,
> Count your many blessings, name them one by one,
> And it will surprise you what the Lord hath done.

In his book *Then Sings My Soul*, Robert Morgan recounts how Howard Rutledge, a captured American soldier in Vietnam, was able to help conquer the loneliness and despair of his long captivity by recalling hymns from childhood. The following is a quote from Rutledge's own book, *In the Presence of Mine Enemies*, describing how he suddenly remembered lines from the hymn *There Shall Be Showers of Blessing* during a heavy monsoon rainstorm:

> I tried desperately to recall . . . gospel choruses from childhood, and hymns we sang in church. The first three dozen songs were relatively easy. Every day I would try to

recall another verse or a new song. One night there was a huge thunderstorm—it was the season of the monsoon rains—and a bolt of lightening knocked out the lights and plunged the entire prison into darkness. I had been going over hymn tunes in my mind and stopped to lie down and sleep when the rains began to fall. The darkened prison echoed with wave after wave of water. Suddenly I was humming my thirty-seventh song, one I had entirely forgotten since childhood.[1]

> Showers of blessing,
> Showers of blessing we need!
> Mercy drops round us are falling,
> But for the showers we plead.

There Shall Be Showers of Blessing was inspired by words spoken by the Lord through the prophet Ezekiel when He said how He would cause showers of blessing to rain down on His people:

> Therefore will I save my flock, and they shall no more be a prey; and I will judge between cattle and cattle. And I will set up one shepherd over them, and he shall feed them, even my servant David; he shall feed them, and he shall be their shepherd. And I the LORD will be their God, and my servant David a prince among them; I the LORD have spoken it. And I will make with them a covenant of peace, and will cause the evil beasts to cease out of the land: and they shall dwell safely in the wilderness, and sleep in the woods. And I will make them and the places round about my hill a blessing; and I will cause the shower to come down in his season; there shall be showers of blessing. (Ezekiel 34:22-26)

Rutledge, the formerly downed soldier, made it clear that scriptural hymns like *There Shall Be Showers of Blessing* were an incredible blessing to him in captivity. As other soldiers lost hope, gave up, and died, he was able to press on and survive.

In this same regard, the hymn *Blessed Assurance* (written by renowned hymnist Fanny Crosby) reminds us that when it is all said and done—whatever our circumstances may be—Jesus Christ is our blessed hope, and He is our ultimate blessing.

> Blessed Assurance, Jesus is mine!
> Oh, what a foretaste of glory divine!
> Heir of salvation, purchase of God,
> Born of His Spirit, washed in His blood.

Scripture tells us that "Every good gift and every perfect gift is from above, and cometh down from the Father of lights, with whom is no variableness, neither shadow of turning" (James 1:17). Thus, we praise God in singing the traditional doxology—recognizing that it is from God that all of our good gifts and blessings flow.

> Praise God from whom all blessings flow.
> Praise Him, all creatures here below.
> Praise Him above, ye heav'nly host.
> Praise Father, Son and Holy Ghost. Amen.

In Robert Robinson's 1757 hymn *Come Thou Fount of Every Blessing*, we are encouraged to sing songs of loudest praise for God's blessings and endless mercies:

> Come, thou fount of every blessing,
> Tune my heart to sing Thy grace.
> Streams of mercy, never ceasing,
> Call for songs of loudest praise.
> Teach me some melodious sonnet,
> Sung by flaming tongues above.
> Praise the mount! I'm fixed upon it,
> Mount of God's unchanging love.

BLESSINGS FROM GOD

BLESSED ARE THOSE WHO TRUST IN GOD

Blessed is the man that trusteth in the LORD, and whose hope the LORD is. For he shall be as a tree planted by the waters, and that spreadeth out her roots by the river, and shall not see when heat cometh, but her leaf shall be green; and shall not be careful in the year of drought, neither shall cease from yielding fruit. (Jeremiah 17:7-8)

O taste and see that the LORD is good: blessed is the man that trusteth in him. (Psalm 34:8)

Blessed is that man that maketh the LORD his trust, and respecteth not the proud, nor such as turn aside to lies. (Psalm 40:4)

O LORD of hosts, blessed is the man that trusteth in thee. (Psalm 84:12)

Serve the LORD with fear, and rejoice with trembling. Kiss the Son, lest he be angry, and ye perish from the way, when his wrath is kindled but a little. Blessed are all they that put their trust in him. (Psalm 2:11-12)

BLESSED ARE THE FAITHFUL

A faithful man shall abound with blessings. (Proverbs 28:20)

Even as Abraham believed God, and it was accounted to him for righteousness. Know ye therefore that they which are of faith, the same are the children of Abraham. And the scripture, foreseeing that God would justify the heathen through faith, preached before the gospel unto Abraham, saying, In thee shall all nations be blessed. So then they which be of faith are blessed with faithful Abraham. (Galatians 3:6-9)

BLESSED ARE THE SEED OF ABRAHAM

Ye are the children of the prophets, and of the covenant which God made with our fathers, saying unto Abraham, And in thy seed shall all the kindreds of the earth be blessed. (Acts 3:25)

BLESSED ARE THOSE WHO FEAR THE LORD

Praise ye the LORD. Blessed is the man that feareth the LORD, that delighteth greatly in his commandments. His seed shall be mighty upon earth: the generation of the upright shall be blessed. (Psalm 112:1-2)

Blessed is every one that feareth the LORD; that walketh in his ways. For thou shalt eat the labour of thine hands: happy shalt thou be, and it shall be well with thee. (Psalm 128:1-2)

Behold, that thus shall the man be blessed that feareth the LORD. The LORD shall bless thee out of Zion: and thou shalt see the good of Jerusalem all the days of thy life. (Psalm 128:4-5)

BLESSED IS THE MAN WHOSE STRENGTH IS GOD

Blessed is the man whose strength is in thee. (Psalm 84:5)

BLESSED ARE THOSE WHO KEEP HIS WAYS

Now therefore hearken unto me, O ye children: for blessed are they that keep my ways. (Proverbs 8:32)

BLESSED ARE THOSE WHO HEAR THE LORD

Hear instruction, and be wise, and refuse it not. Blessed is the man that heareth me, watching daily at my gates, waiting at the posts of my doors. (Proverbs 8:33-34)

BLESSED ARE THOSE WHO WALK IN GOD'S LAW

Blessed are the undefiled in the way, who walk in the law of the LORD. (Psalm 119:1)

BLESSED ARE THOSE WHO HEAR GOD'S WORD AND KEEP IT

But he said, Yea rather, blessed are they that hear the word of God, and keep it. (Luke 11:28)

BLESSED ARE THOSE WHO KEEP HIS COMMANDMENTS

Behold, I set before you this day a blessing and a curse; A blessing, if ye obey the commandments of the LORD your God, which I command you this day: And a curse, if ye will not obey the commandments of the LORD your God, but turn aside out of the way which I command you this day, to go after other gods, which ye have not known. (Deuteronomy 11:26-28)

BLESSED ARE THOSE WHO KEEP HIS TESTIMONIES

Blessed are they that keep his testimonies, and that seek him with the whole heart. (Psalm 119:2)

BLESSED ARE THOSE WHOSE SINS ARE FORGIVEN

Blessed is he whose transgression is forgiven, whose sin is covered. (Psalm 32:1)

BLESSED ARE THOSE TO WHOM SIN IS NOT IMPUTED

Blessed is the man unto whom the LORD imputeth not iniquity, and in whose spirit there is no guile. (Psalm 32:2)

Blessed is the man to whom the Lord will not impute sin. (Romans 4:8)

BLESSED ARE THE POOR IN SPIRIT

Blessed are the poor in spirit: for theirs is the kingdom of heaven. (Matthew 5:3)

BLESSED ARE THEY THAT MOURN

Blessed are they that mourn: for they shall be comforted. (Matthew 5:4)

BLESSED ARE THE MEEK

Blessed are the meek: for they shall inherit the earth. (Matthew 5:5)

BLESSED ARE THEY THAT HUNGER AFTER RIGHTEOUSNESS

Blessed are they which do hunger and thirst after righteousness: for they shall be filled. (Matthew 5:6)

BLESSED ARE THE MERCIFUL

Blessed are the merciful: for they shall obtain mercy. (Matthew 5:7)

BLESSED ARE THE PURE IN HEART

Blessed are the pure in heart: for they shall see God. (Matthew 5:8)

BLESSED ARE THE PEACEMAKERS

Blessed are the peacemakers: for they shall be called the children of God. (Matthew 5:9)

BLESSED ARE THEY THAT ARE PERSECUTED

Blessed are they which are persecuted for righteousness' sake: for theirs is the kingdom of heaven. (Matthew 5:10)

Blessed are ye, when men shall revile you, and persecute you, and shall say all manner of evil against you falsely, for my sake. Rejoice, and be exceeding glad: for great is your reward in heaven: for so persecuted they the prophets which were before you. (Matthew 5:11-12)

BLESSED ARE THOSE WHO ARE HATED

Blessed are ye, when men shall hate you, and when they shall separate you from their company, and shall reproach you, and cast out your name as evil, for the Son of man's sake. Rejoice ye in that day, and leap for joy: for, behold, your reward is great in heaven: for in the like manner did their fathers unto the prophets. (Luke 6:22-23)

BLESSED ARE THOSE WHO ARE NOT OFFENDED

And blessed is he, whosoever shall not be offended in me. (Matthew 11:6)

BLESSED ARE THOSE WHO ENDURE TEMPTATION

Blessed is the man that endureth temptation: for when he is tried, he shall receive the crown of life, which the Lord hath promised to them that love him. (James 1:12)

BLESSED ARE THOSE WHO GIVE

I have showed you all things, how that so labouring ye ought to support the weak, and to remember the words of the Lord Jesus, how he said, It is more blessed to give than to receive. (Acts 20:35)

BLESSED ARE THOSE WHO CONSIDER THE POOR AND THE UNFORTUNATE

Blessed is he that considereth the poor: the LORD will deliver him in time of trouble. The LORD will preserve him, and keep him alive; and he shall be blessed upon the earth: and thou wilt not deliver him unto the will of his enemies. (Psalm 41:1-2)

Then said he also to him that bade him, When thou makest a dinner or a supper, call not thy friends, nor thy brethren, neither thy kinsmen, nor thy rich neighbours; lest they also bid thee again, and a recompense be made thee. But when thou makest a feast, call the poor, the maimed, the lame, the blind: And thou shalt be blessed; for they cannot recompense thee: for thou shalt be recompensed at the resurrection of the just. And when one of them that sat at meat with him heard these things, he said unto him, Blessed is he that shall eat bread in the kingdom of God. (Luke 14:12-15)

BLESSED ARE THOSE WHO ARE CHASTENED BY THE LORD

Blessed is the man whom thou chastenest, O LORD, and teachest him out of thy law. (Psalm 94:12)

BLESSED ARE THOSE WHO KEEP JUDGMENT

Blessed are they that keep judgment, and he that doeth righteousness at all times. (Psalm 106:3)

Thus saith the LORD, Keep ye judgment, and do justice: for my salvation is near to come, and my righteousness to be revealed. Blessed is the man that doeth this, and the son of man that layeth hold on it. (Isaiah 56:1-2)

BLESSED ARE THOSE WHO DWELL IN THE HOUSE OF THE LORD

Blessed are they that dwell in thy house: they will be still praising thee. (Psalm 84:4)

BLESSED ARE THOSE WHO HAVE NOT SEEN THE LORD BUT BELIEVE

Then saith he to Thomas, Reach hither thy finger, and behold my hands; and reach hither thy hand, and thrust it into my side: and be not faithless, but believing. And Thomas answered and said unto him, My Lord and my God. Jesus saith unto him, Thomas, because thou hast seen me, thou hast believed: blessed are they that have not seen, and yet have believed. (John 20:27-29)

BLESSED ARE THOSE WHO RECEIVE SPIRITUAL BLESSINGS IN HEAVENLY PLACES IN CHRIST

Blessed be the God and Father of our Lord Jesus Christ, who hath blessed us with all spiritual blessings in heavenly places in Christ: According as he hath chosen us in him before the foundation of the world, that we should be holy and without blame before him in love. (Ephesians 1:3-4)

BLESSED IS THE GOSPEL OF CHRIST

And I am sure that, when I come unto you, I shall come in the fulness of the blessing of the gospel of Christ. (Romans 15:29)

BLESSED ARE THE JUST

Blessings are upon the head of the just: but violence covereth the mouth of the wicked. (Proverbs 10:6)

BLESSED ARE THE DOERS

But whoso looketh into the perfect law of liberty, and continueth therein, he being not a forgetful hearer, but a doer of the work, this man shall be blessed in his deed. (James 1:25)

BLESSED ARE THOSE WHO DON'T WALK IN THE COUNSEL OF THE UNGODLY

Blessed is the man that walketh not in the counsel of the ungodly, nor standeth in the way of sinners, nor sitteth in the seat of the scornful. But his delight is in the law of the LORD; and in his law doth he meditate day and night. And he shall be like a tree planted by the rivers of water, that bringeth forth his fruit in his season; his leaf also shall not wither; and whatsoever he doeth shall prosper. (Psalm 1:1-3)

BLESSED ARE THE PEOPLE WHO KNOW JUSTICE, JUDGMENT, MERCY, AND TRUTH

Thou hast a mighty arm: strong is thy hand, and high is thy right hand. Justice and judgment are the habitation of thy throne: mercy and truth shall go before thy face. Blessed is the people that know the joyful sound: they shall walk, O LORD, in the light of thy countenance. (Psalm 89:13-15)

BLESSED ARE THOSE WHO ARE WITH THE ONE SHEPHERD

And I will set up one shepherd over them, and he shall feed them, even my servant David; he shall feed them, and he shall be their shepherd. . . . And I will make them and the places round about my hill a blessing; and I will cause the shower to come down in his season; there shall be showers of blessing. (Ezekiel 34:23, 26)

BLESSED IS THE NATION WHOSE GOD IS THE LORD

Blessed is the nation whose God is the LORD; and the people whom he hath chosen for his own inheritance. (Psalm 33:12)

THE SEVEN REVELATION BLESSINGS

BLESSED ARE THOSE THAT READ, HEAR, AND KEEP THE REVELATION OF JESUS CHRIST

The Revelation of Jesus Christ, which God gave unto him, to show unto his servants things which must shortly come to pass; and he sent and signified it by his angel unto his servant John: Who bare record of the word of God, and of the testimony of Jesus Christ, and of all things that he saw. Blessed is he that readeth, and they that hear the words of this prophecy, and keep those things which are written therein: for the time is at hand. (Revelation 1:1-3)

BLESSED ARE THOSE WHO DIE IN THE LORD HENCEFORTH

And I heard a voice from heaven saying unto me, Write, Blessed are the dead which die in the Lord from henceforth: Yea, saith the Spirit, that they may rest from their labours; and their works do follow them. (Revelation 14:13)

BLESSED ARE THOSE WHO WATCH AND KEEP THEIR GARMENTS

Behold, I come as a thief. Blessed is he that watcheth, and keepeth his garments, lest he walk naked, and they see his shame. (Revelation 16:15)

BLESSED ARE THOSE CALLED TO THE MARRIAGE SUPPER

And he saith unto me, Write, Blessed are they which are called unto the marriage supper of the Lamb. And he saith unto me, These are the true sayings of God. (Revelation 19:9)

BLESSED ARE THOSE THAT ARE PART OF THE FIRST RESURRECTION

And I saw thrones, and they sat upon them, and judgment was given unto them: and I saw the souls of them that were beheaded for the witness of Jesus, and for the word of God, and which had not worshipped the beast, neither his image, neither had received his mark upon their foreheads, or in their hands; and they lived and reigned with Christ a thousand years. But the rest of the dead lived not again until the thousand years were finished. This is the first resurrection. Blessed and holy is he that hath part in the first resurrection: on such the second death hath no power, but they shall be priests of God and of Christ, and shall reign with him a thousand years. (Revelation 20:4-6)

BLESSED ARE THOSE WHO KEEP THE SAYINGS OF THIS BOOK

And he said unto me, These sayings are faithful and true: and the Lord God of the holy prophets sent his angel to shew unto his servants the things which must shortly be done. Behold, I come quickly: blessed is he that keepeth the sayings of the prophecy of this book. (Revelation 22:6-7)

BLESSED ARE THOSE WHO KEEP GOD'S COMMANDMENTS

And, behold, I come quickly; and my reward is with me, to give every man according as his work shall be. I am Alpha and Omega, the beginning and the end, the first and the last. Blessed are they that do his commandments, that they may have right to the tree of life, and may enter in through the gates into the city. (Revelation 22:12-14)

JESUS CHRIST—OUR BLESSED HOPE

BLESSED ARE THOSE WHO WAIT

And therefore will the LORD wait, that he may be gracious unto you, and therefore will he be exalted, that he may have mercy upon you: for the LORD is a God of judgment: blessed are all they that wait for him. (Isaiah 30:18)

And from the time that the daily sacrifice shall be taken away, and the abomination that maketh desolate set up, there shall be a thousand two hundred and ninety days. Blessed is he that waiteth, and cometh to the thousand three hundred and five and thirty days. (Daniel 12:11-12)

BLESSED ARE THOSE WHO WAIT AND WATCH FOR THE LORD

Let your loins be girded about, and your lights burning; And ye yourselves like unto men that wait for their lord, when he will return from the wedding; that when he cometh and knocketh, they may open unto him immediately. Blessed are those servants, whom the lord when he cometh shall find watching: verily I say unto you, that he shall gird himself, and make them to sit down to meat, and will come forth and serve them. (Luke 12:35-37)

And if he shall come in the second watch, or come in the third watch, and find them so, blessed are those servants. And this know, that if the goodman of the house had known what hour the thief would come, he would have watched, and not have suffered his house to be broken through. Be ye therefore ready also: for the Son of man cometh at an hour when ye think not. (Luke 12:38-40)

For the grace of God that bringeth salvation hath appeared to all men, Teaching us that, denying ungodliness and worldly lusts, we should live soberly, righteously, and godly, in this present world; Looking for that blessed hope, and the glorious appearing of the great God and our Saviour Jesus Christ; Who gave himself for us, that he might redeem us from all iniquity, and purify unto himself a peculiar people, zealous of good works. These things speak, and exhort, and rebuke with all authority. Let no man despise thee. (Titus 2:11-15)

BLESSINGS THROUGH IT ALL

While God promises that blessings accompany our faith in Him, we are also promised hatred and persecution from the world. However, the blessed assurance of our faith in Jesus Christ enables us to endure and persevere through it all.

CHAPTER FOURTEEN

PRAISING GOD THROUGH IT ALL

Make a joyful noise unto the LORD, all ye lands. Serve the LORD with gladness: come before his presence with singing. Know ye that the LORD he is God: it is he that hath made us, and not we ourselves; we are his people, and the sheep of his pasture. Enter into his gates with thanksgiving, and into his courts with praise: be thankful unto him, and bless his name. For the Lord is good; his mercy is everlasting; and his truth endureth to all generations. (Psalm 100:1-5)

OUR PRAISE TO GOD

But thou art holy, O thou that inhabitest the praises of Israel. (Psalm 22:3)

Our praise unto God is our acknowledgment of everything He has done, is doing, and will continue to do in our lives (Psalm 107:31). He created the heavens and the earth (Genesis 2:4). He created mankind (Genesis 1:27). He created every living creature that moves (Genesis 1:21). He created all things (Colossians 1:16). He sent His Son Jesus Christ to be our Lord and Savior to save us from our sins (Matthew 1:21). Jesus defeated sin, death, and a very real Satan on the Cross of Calvary (Hebrews 2:14). To those who believe in Him, He has given the gift of everlasting life (John 3:16). We are eternally grateful (1 Thessalonians 5:18). What more could He have possibly done (Isaiah 5:4)? Therefore, we want to praise Him in all we say and do (Psalm 71:8).

Our praise is to be proclaimed continually (Hebrews 13:15-16). It is to be offered both in good times and in bad (Psalm 34:1) because He is always faithful (2 Thessalonians 3:3), and He is always true (Revelation 3:7). He is God, and there is none beside Him (Isaiah 45:22). His merciful kindness is great towards us, and His truth endures forever (Psalm 117:2). He promised He would never leave us or forsake us (Hebrews 13:5) and would be with us even to the end of the world (Matthew 28:20). It is no wonder Scripture tells us that God is to be exalted "above the heavens" (Psalm 57:5). He is "holy" (Psalm 99:5); He is "good" (Psalm 135:3); He is "great" (Psalm 145:3); and He is "worthy to be praised" (2 Samuel 22:4). As believers, our desire should be to praise God with our song (Psalm 28:7), with our lives (Psalm 146:2), and with our every breath (Psalm 150:6).

HYMNS OF PRAISE TO HIM

An important part of our praising God is with psalms, hymns, and songs (Colossians 3:16). *Praise Him, Praise Him* (1869) is poetess Fanny Crosby's beloved hymn to our Lord and Savior. The hymnist tells us to "sound" our praises to Jesus, our blessed Redeemer:

> Praise Him! Praise Him! Jesus, our blessed Redeemer!
> For our sins He suffered, and bled, and died;
> He's our Rock, our hope of eternal salvation,
> Hail Him! Hail Him! Jesus the crucified.
> Sound His praises! Jesus who bore our sorrows,

Love unbounded, wonderful, deep, and strong.

Praise Him! praise Him!
Tell of His excellent greatness,
Praise Him! praise Him!
Ever in joyful song!

In another Crosby hymn, *Blessed Assurance* (1873), her powerful words of praise have echoed through church sanctuaries and resounded in people's hearts for well over a century:

Blessed assurance, Jesus is mine!
Oh what a foretaste of glory divine!
Heir of salvation, purchase of God,
Born of His Spirit, washed in His blood.
This is my story, this is my song.
Praising my Saviour all the day long;
This is my story, this is my song,
Praising my Saviour all the day long.

In *O, For a Heart to Praise My God* (1742), hymn writer Charles Wesley yearns for a heart to praise God:

O, for a heart to praise my God,
A heart from sin set free,
A heart that always feels Thy blood,
So freely shed for me.

In another hymn, *Come, Thou Almighty King*, Wesley again beseeches God for help in our praise of Him:

Come, Thou Almighty King,
Help us Thy name to sing,
Help us to praise: Father, all glorious,
O'r all victorious,

Come, and reign over us,
Ancient of Days.

Psalm 148 exhorts all creation to praise the Lord from the heavens and the heights:

Praise ye the Lord.
Praise ye the Lord from the heavens:
Praise him in the heights.
Praise ye him, all his angels:
Praise ye him, all his hosts.
Praise ye him, sun and moon:
Praise him, all ye stars of light.
Praise him, ye heavens of heavens,
And ye waters that be above the heavens.
Let them praise the name of the Lord:
For he commanded, and they were created. (vs. 1-5)

Obviously echoing this psalm is *Praise God From Whom All Blessings Flow* from the 17th century by Thomas Ken:

Praise God, from Whom all blessings flow;
Praise Him, all creatures here below;
Praise Him above, ye heavenly host;
Praise Father, Son, and Holy Ghost.

All too often, however, in the midst of our busy lives, we forget the Lord and the importance of heartfelt praise. When we take the time to reflect on what the Bible says about praise, we are encouraged to give God the praise that most assuredly is His due (Psalm 29:2). The Bible is very explicit on who gives Him praise, why we give Him praise, how we give Him praise, and where and when we give Him praise.

WHO PRAISES GOD?

THE HEAVENS

And the heavens shall praise thy wonders, O LORD: thy faithfulness also in the congregation of the saints. (Psalm 89:5)

ALL PEOPLE

Let the people praise thee, O God; let all the people praise thee. (Psalm 67:3)

ALL NATIONS

O Praise the LORD, all ye nations: praise him, all ye people. (Psalm 117:1)

ALL CREATION

Praise ye the LORD. Praise ye the LORD from the heavens: praise him in the heights. Praise ye him, all his angels: praise ye him, all his hosts. Praise ye him, sun and moon: praise him, all ye stars of light. Praise him, ye heavens of heavens, and ye waters that be above the heavens. Let them praise the name of the LORD: for he commanded, and they were created. (Psalm 148:1-5)

THE SHEEP OF HIS PASTURE

So we thy people and sheep of thy pasture will give thee thanks for ever: we will show forth thy praise to all generations. (Psalm 79:13)

THE MEEK

The meek shall eat and be satisfied: they shall praise the LORD that seek him: your heart shall live for ever. (Psalm 22:26)

THE POOR AND THE NEEDY

O let not the oppressed return ashamed: let the poor and needy praise thy name. (Psalm 74:21)

EVERYTHING THAT MOVES

Let the heaven and earth praise him, the seas, and every thing that moveth therein. (Psalm 69:34)

EVERYTHING THAT HAS BREATH

Let every thing that hath breath praise the LORD. Praise ye the LORD. (Psalm 150:6)

WHY DO WE PRAISE GOD?

BECAUSE IT GLORIFIES GOD

Whoso offereth praise glorifieth me: and to him that ordereth his conversation aright will I show the salvation of God. (Psalm 50:23)

BECAUSE HE IS OUR PRAISE

Thou shalt fear the LORD thy God; him shalt thou serve, and to him shalt thou cleave, and swear by his name. He is thy praise, and he is thy God, that hath done for thee these great and terrible things, which thine eyes have seen. (Deuteronomy 10:20-21)

BECAUSE PRAISE IS COMELY

Rejoice in the LORD, O ye righteous: for praise is comely for the upright. (Psalm 33:1)

BECAUSE PRAISE IS GOOD

Praise ye the LORD: for it is good to sing praises unto our God; for it is pleasant; and praise is comely. (Psalm 147:1)

BECAUSE GOD IS GOOD

Praise the LORD; for the LORD is good: sing praises unto his name; for it is pleasant. (Psalm 135:3)

BECAUSE GOD IS GREAT

Great is the LORD, and greatly to be praised; and his greatness is unsearchable. (Psalm 145:3)

BECAUSE GOD IS WORTHY

I will call on the LORD, who is worthy to be praised: so shall I be saved from mine enemies. (2 Samuel 22:4)

BECAUSE OF GOD'S GRACE

To the praise of the glory of his grace, wherein he hath made us accepted in the beloved. In whom we have redemption through his blood, the forgiveness of sins, according to the riches of his grace. (Ephesians 1:6-7)

BECAUSE OF HIS RIGHTEOUSNESS

I will praise the LORD according to his righteousness: and will sing praise to the name of the LORD most high. (Psalm 7:17)

BECAUSE OF GOD'S WORD

In God will I praise his word: in the LORD will I praise his word. (Psalm 56:10)

BECAUSE OF GOD'S NAME

Praise ye the LORD. Praise, O ye servants of the LORD, praise the name of the LORD. (Psalm 113:1)

BECAUSE GOD'S NAME IS HOLY

Let them praise thy great and terrible name; for it is holy. (Psalm 99:3)

BECAUSE GOD'S NAME IS GOOD

I will freely sacrifice unto thee: I will praise thy name, O LORD; for it is good. (Psalm 54:6)

BECAUSE GOD'S NAME IS EXCELLENT

Let them praise the name of the LORD: for his name alone is excellent; his glory is above the earth and heaven. (Psalm 148:13)

BECAUSE OF GOD'S POWER

Be thou exalted, LORD, in thine own strength: so will we sing and praise thy power. (Psalm 21:13)

BECAUSE OF GOD'S HOLINESS

And when he had consulted with the people, he appointed singers unto the LORD, and that should praise the beauty of holiness, as they went out before the army, and to say, Praise the LORD; for his mercy endureth for ever. (2 Chronicles 20:21)

BECAUSE OF GOD'S KINDNESS

O Praise the LORD, all ye nations: praise him, all ye people. For his merciful kindness is great toward us: and the truth of the LORD endureth for ever. Praise ye the LORD. (Psalm 117:1-2)

BECAUSE OF GOD'S LOVINGKINDESS AND TRUTH

Because thy lovingkindness is better than life, my lips shall praise thee. (Psalm 63:3)

I will worship toward thy holy temple, and praise thy name for thy lovingkindness and for thy truth: for thou hast magnified thy word above all thy name. (Psalm 138:2)

BECAUSE OF GOD'S MERCY AND TRUTH

I will praise thee, O LORD, among the people: and I will sing praises unto thee among the nations. For thy mercy is great above the heavens: and thy truth reacheth unto the clouds. (Psalm 108:3-4)

BECAUSE GOD'S MERCY ENDURETH FOREVER

Praise ye the LORD. O give thanks unto the LORD; for he is good: for his mercy endureth for ever. (Psalm 106:1)

And when all the children of Israel saw how the fire came down, and the glory of the LORD upon the house, they bowed themselves with their faces to the ground upon the pavement, and worshipped, and praised the LORD, saying, For he is good; for his mercy endureth for ever. (2 Chronicles 7:3)

The voice of joy, and the voice of gladness, the voice of the bridegroom, and the voice of the bride, the voice of them that shall say, Praise the LORD of hosts: for the LORD is good; for his mercy endureth for ever. (Jeremiah 33:11)

BECAUSE GOD IS THE HEALTH OF OUR COUNTENANCE

Why art thou cast down, O my soul? and why art thou disquieted within me? hope thou in God: for I shall yet praise him, who is the health of my countenance, and my God. (Psalm 42:11)

BECAUSE GOD SET OUR FEET UPON A ROCK

I waited patiently for the LORD; and he inclined unto me, and heard my cry. He brought me up also out of an horrible pit, out of the miry clay, and set my feet upon a rock, and established my goings. And he hath put a new song in my mouth, even praise unto our God: many shall see it, and fear, and shall trust in the LORD. (Psalm 40:1-3)

BECAUSE OF GOD'S WONDERFUL WORKS

Oh that men would praise the LORD for his goodness, and for his wonderful works to the children of men! (Psalm 107:31)

BECAUSE GOD CALLED US OUT OF DARKNESS

But ye are a chosen generation, a royal priesthood, an holy nation, a peculiar people; that ye should show forth the praises of him who hath called you out of darkness into his marvellous light. (1 Peter 2:9)

BECAUSE GOD SAVES US FROM OUR ENEMIES

But thou hast saved us from our enemies, and hast put them to shame that hated us. In God we boast all the day long, and praise thy name for ever. (Psalm 44:7-8)

BECAUSE GOD SENT US A SAVIOR

For unto you is born this day in the city of David a Saviour, which is Christ the Lord. And this shall be a sign unto you; Ye shall find the babe wrapped in swaddling clothes, lying in a manger. And suddenly there was with the angel a multitude of the heavenly host praising God, and saying, Glory to God in the highest, and on earth peace, good will toward men. (Luke 2:11-14)

BECAUSE GOD IS OUR SALVATION

I will praise thee: for thou hast heard me, and art become my salvation. The stone which the builders refused is become the head stone of the corner. (Psalm 118:21-22)

HOW DO WE PRAISE GOD?

WE PRAISE GOD WITH THE SACRIFICE OF PRAISE

By him therefore let us offer the sacrifice of praise to God continually, that is, the fruit of our lips giving thanks to his name. (Hebrews 13:15)

WE PRAISE GOD WITH GLORIOUS PRAISE

Make a joyful noise unto God, all ye lands: Sing forth the honour of his name: make his praise glorious. (Psalm 66:1-2)

WE PRAISE GOD WITH A FIXED HEART

O God, my heart is fixed; I will sing and give praise, even with my glory. (Psalm 108:1)

My heart is fixed, O God, my heart is fixed: I will sing and give praise. (Psalm 57:7)

WE PRAISE GOD WITH UPRIGHTNESS OF HEART

I will praise thee with uprightness of heart, when I shall have learned thy righteous judgments. (Psalm 119:7)

WE PRAISE GOD WITH OUR WHOLE HEART

I will praise thee, O LORD, with my whole heart; I will show forth all thy marvellous works. (Psalm 9:1)

Praise ye the LORD. I will praise the LORD with my whole heart, in the assembly of the upright, and in the congregation. (Psalm 111:1)

I will praise thee, O Lord my God, with all my heart: and I will glorify thy name for evermore. (Psalm 86:12)

WE PRAISE GOD WITH GLADNESS

Moreover Hezekiah the king and the princes commanded the Levites to sing praise unto the LORD with the words of David, and of Asaph the seer. And they sang praises with gladness, and they bowed their heads and worshipped. (2 Chronicles 29:30)

WE PRAISE GOD WITH THANKFULNESS

It is a good thing to give thanks unto the LORD, and to sing praises unto thy name, O most High. (Psalm 92:1)

And he appointed certain of the Levites to minister before the ark of the LORD, and to record, and to thank and praise the LORD God of Israel. (1 Chronicles 16:4)

And the chief of the Levites: Hashabiah, Sherebiah, and Jeshua the son of Kadmiel, with their brethren over against them, to praise and to give thanks, according to the commandment of David the man of God, ward over against ward. (Nehemiah 12:24)

And when the builders laid the foundation of the temple of the LORD, they set the priests in their apparel with trumpets, and the Levites the sons of Asaph with cymbals, to praise the LORD, after the ordinance of David king of Israel. And they sang together by course in praising and giving thanks unto the LORD; because he is good, for his mercy endureth for ever toward Israel. And all the people shouted with a great shout, when they praised the LORD, because the foundation of the house of the LORD was laid. (Ezra 3:10-11)

Thine, O LORD, is the greatness, and the power, and the glory, and the victory, and the majesty: for all that is in the heaven and in the earth is thine; thine is the kingdom, O LORD, and thou art exalted as head above all. Both riches and honour come of thee, and thou reignest over all; and in thine hand is power and might; and in thine hand it is to make great, and to give strength unto all. Now therefore, our God, we thank thee, and praise thy glorious name. (1 Chronicles 29:11-13)

WE PRAISE GOD WITH A JOYFUL NOISE

Make a joyful noise unto the LORD, all the earth: make a loud noise, and rejoice, and sing praise. (Psalm 98:4)

WE PRAISE GOD WITH JOYFUL LIPS

My soul shall be satisfied as with marrow and fatness; and my mouth shall praise thee with joyful lips. When I remember thee upon my bed, and meditate on thee in the night watches. Because thou hast been my help, therefore in the shadow of thy wings will I rejoice. (Psalm 63:5-7)

WE PRAISE GOD WITH SINGING

Therefore will I give thanks unto thee, O LORD, among the heathen, and sing praises unto thy name. (Psalm 18:49)

I will praise thee, O LORD, among the people: and I will sing praises unto thee among the nations. For thy mercy is great above the heavens: and thy truth reacheth unto the clouds. (Psalm 108:3-4)

For God is the King of all the earth: sing ye praises with understanding. (Psalm 47:7)

The LORD is my strength and my shield; my heart trusted in him, and I am helped: therefore my heart greatly rejoiceth; and with my song will I praise him. (Psalm 28:7)

WE PRAISE GOD WITH DANCE

Let them praise his name in the dance: let them sing praises unto him with the timbrel and harp. For the LORD taketh pleasure in his people: he will beautify the meek with salvation. (Psalm 149:3-4)

WE PRAISE THE LORD WITH MUSICAL INSTRUMENTS

Praise the LORD with harp: sing unto him with the psaltery and an instrument of ten strings. (Psalm 33:2)

Praise him with the sound of the trumpet: praise him with the psaltery and harp. Praise him with the timbrel and dance: praise him with stringed instruments and organs. Praise him upon the loud cymbals: praise him upon the high sounding cymbals. (Psalm 150:3-5)

WE PRAISE GOD BY MAKING OUR PRAISE HEARD

O bless our God, ye people, and make the voice of his praise to be heard. (Psalm 66:8)

WHERE DO WE PRAISE GOD?

WE PRAISE GOD AMONG THE NATIONS

I will praise thee, O Lord, among the people: I will sing unto thee among the nations. (Psalm 57:9)

WE PRAISE GOD AMONG THE MULTITUDE

I will greatly praise the LORD with my mouth; yea, I will praise him among the multitude. For he shall stand at the right hand of the poor, to save him from those that condemn his soul. (Psalm 109:30-31)

WE PRAISE GOD AMONG THE PEOPLE

I will praise thee among much people. (Psalm 35:18)

WE PRAISE GOD IN HIS SANCTUARY

Praise ye the LORD. Praise God in his sanctuary: praise him in the firmament of his power. (Psalm 150:1)

WE PRAISE GOD IN THE CONGREGATION

I will declare thy name unto my brethren: in the midst of the congregation will I praise thee. (Psalm 22:22)

My praise shall be of thee in the great congregation: I will pay my vows before them that fear him. (Psalm 22:25)

Praise ye the LORD. Sing unto the LORD a new song, and his praise in the congregation of saints. (Psalm 149:1)

WE PRAISE GOD IN THE MIDST OF THE CHURCH

Saying, I will declare thy name unto my brethren, in the midst of the church will I sing praise unto thee. (Hebrews 2:12)

WE PRAISE GOD WHEN WE ENTER HIS COURTS

Enter into his gates with thanksgiving, and into his courts with praise: be thankful unto him, and bless his name. For the LORD is good; his mercy is everlasting; and his truth endureth to all generations. (Psalm 100:4-5)

WHEN DO WE PRAISE GOD?

WE PRAISE GOD IN ALL THINGS

If any man speak, let him speak as the oracles of God; if any man minister, let him do it as of the ability which God giveth: that God in all things may be glorified through Jesus Christ, to whom be praise and dominion for ever and ever. Amen. (1 Peter 4:11)

WE PRAISE GOD FROM THIS TIME FORTH

But we will bless the LORD from this time forth and for evermore. Praise the LORD. (Psalm 115:18)

WE PRAISE GOD CONTINUALLY

I will bless the LORD at all times: his praise shall continually be in my mouth. (Psalm 34:1)

For thou art my hope, O Lord GOD: thou art my trust from my youth. By thee have I been holden up from the womb: thou art he that took me out of my mother's bowels: my praise shall be continually of thee. (Psalm 71:5-6)

WE PRAISE GOD MORE AND MORE

But I will hope continually, and will yet praise thee more and more. (Psalm 71:14)

WE PRAISE GOD SEVEN TIMES A DAY

Seven times a day do I praise thee because of thy righteous judgments. (Psalm 119:164)

WE PRAISE GOD ALL DAY LONG

And my tongue shall speak of thy righteousness and of thy praise all the day long. (Psalm 35:28)

Let my mouth be filled with thy praise and with thy honour all the day. (Psalm 71:8)

From the rising of the sun unto the going down of the same the Lord's name is to be praised. (Psalm 113:3)

WE PRAISE GOD AS LONG AS WE LIVE

I will sing unto the LORD as long as I live: I will sing praise to my God while I have my being. (Psalm 104:33)

Praise ye the LORD. Praise the LORD, O my soul. While I live will I praise the LORD: I will sing praises unto my God while I have any being. (Psalm 146:1-2)

WE PRAISE GOD FOREVER

Every day will I bless thee; and I will praise thy name for ever and ever. (Psalm 145:2)

In God we boast all the day long, and praise thy name for ever. (Psalm 44:8)

I will praise thee for ever, because thou hast done it: and I will wait on thy name; for it is good before thy saints. (Psalm 52:9)

AMAZING PRAISE

The Bible is replete with countless examples of how we are to rejoice, give thanks, and praise God in all circumstances and for ever more. Especially as the days grow darker, may we always remember that we are just that much closer to Jesus' return. So let our light shine and let our faith in Him be evident to all those whom we meet along the way. And may our praises ring out into the world and echo forth into all eternity. The last stanza of John Newton's *Amazing Grace* (1779) says it all:

When we've been there ten thousand years,
Bright shining as the sun,
We've no less days to sing God's praise
Than when we first begun.

PRAYER FOR PRAISE
Fill Thou My Life, O Lord My God
Fill Thou my life, O Lord my God,
In every part with praise,
That my whole being may proclaim
Thy being and Thy ways.

Not for the lip of praise alone,
Nor for the praising heart;
I ask Thee for a life made up
Of praise in every part.

Praise in the common things of life,
It's goings out and in;
Praise in each duty and each deed,
However small and mean.

Fill every part of me with praise;
Let all my being speak

Of Thee and of Thy love, O Lord,
Poor though I be, and weak.

So shalt Thou, Lord, from me, even me,
Receive the glory due;
And so shall I begin on earth
The song forever new.

So shall no part of day or night
From sacredness be free:
But all my life, in every step,
Be fellowship with thee.

—Horatius Bonar (1808-1889)

PRAISE GOD AND PRESS ON

And so, with God's help and God's Word, we endeavour to stand fast and press on—through it all—to the higher calling of our Lord and Savior Jesus Christ.

I press toward the mark for the prize of the high calling of God in Christ Jesus. (Philippians 3:14)

ENDNOTES

CHAPTER ONE

1. D. L. Moody, *Prevailing Prayer: What Hinders It,* (Chicago, IL: F.H. Revell, 1884), p. 5.
2. E. M. Bounds, *The Complete Works of E. M. Bounds on Prayer* (Grand Rapids, MI: Baker Books, 1990), p. 66.
3. Ibid., p. 39.
4. Ibid.

CHAPTER THREE

1. Harry Ironside, "Exposing Error: Is It Worthwhile?" (public domain; you may view the entire article at www.lighthousetrails.com/ironside-error.pdf).

CHAPTER SIX

1. Isaac Watts, *O God, Our Help In Ages Past,* 1719. Public domain.
2. Edward Mote, *My Hope is Built on Nothing Less,* 1834. Public domain.
3. Keith Getty and Stuart Townsend, *In Christ Alone,* Copyright © 2002 Thankyou Music (PRS), (adm. worldwide at CapitolCMGPublishing.com excluding Europe which is adm. by Integritymusic.com) All rights reserved. Used by permission.

CHAPTER THIRTEEN

1. Robert J. Morgan, *Then Sings My Soul Book 2* (Nashville TN: Thomas Nelson, Inc., 2004), p. 193.

OTHER BOOKS BY WARREN B. SMITH

The Light That Was Dark: From the New Age to Amazing Grace

False Christ Coming—Does Anybody Care?: What New Age Leaders Really Have in Store for America, the Church, and the World

Deceived on Purpose: The New Age Implications of the Purpose-Driven Church

A "Wonderful" Deception: The Further New Age Implications of the Emerging Purpose Driven Movement

"Another Jesus" Calling: How Sarah Young's False Christ is Deceiving the Church

Watering the Greyhound Garden: Stories From the Streets of San Francisco

Each of these books sells for $14.95 and are available through most major online book outlets and can also be ordered through most bookstores. Wholesale orders call Bookmasters at: (877) 312-3520.

DVDS AND BOOKLETS BY WARREN B. SMITH

LECTURE DVDS
Quantum Lie: God is NOT in Everything
Three Talks in Bend, Oregon
Standing Fast in the Last Days

TOPICAL BOOKLETS
The New Age Implications of Jesus Calling
Changing Jesus Calling: Damage Control for a False Christ
10 Scriptural Reasons Jesus Calling is a Dangerous Book
Rick Warren's Daniel Plan
The Shack and Its New Age Leaven
Remaining Hopeful Through It All
The Awesome Wonder of God's Word
Being Thankful Through It All
Praising God Through it All
Be Still and Know That You Are Not God
Truth or Consequences
False Revival Coming: Holy Laughter or Strong Delusion
Rejoicing Through It All
Blessings Through It All
Remaining Faithful Through It All
Standing Fast Through It All
Trusting God Through It All
Oprah Winfrey's New Age Christianity - Part 1
Oprah Winfrey's New Age Christianity - Part 2
Sound Doctrine Through It All
Help and Comfort Through It All
Leonard Sweet (A More Magnificent Way)

Order all of the above from Lighthouse Trails (866) 876-3910.
For a complete listing of Warren B. Smith's books, booklets, DVDs, and articles, visit his website at www.warrenbsmith.com. Warren's books and booklets are also available in Kindle epub format.

You may write to Warren at:
Mountain Stream Press
Warren B. Smith
P.O. Box 1794
Magalia, CA 95954

E-mail: warren@mountainstreampress.org.
You may visit Warren's website at:
www.warrenbsmith.com.

Notes

Made in the USA
Lexington, KY
22 September 2017